You M NOW STO BELIEVING IT

You Made it Up, NOW STOP BELIEVING IT

The Powerful Body Memory Process for Childhood Vow Discovery and Release

KATHI SOHN

Foreword by Dr. John Degarmo
Founder of the Foster Care Institute

Published by Body Memory Process, LLC
Website: https://bodymemoryprocess.com

ISBN (paperback): 979-8-218-18660-9
ISBN (ebook): 979-8-218-18659-3

Book design: Christy Day, Constellation Book Services

Printed in the United States of America

The remedies, approaches, and techniques described herein are meant to supplement, and not to be a substitute for, professional medical care or treatment.

The first names of Body Memory Process clients referenced in this book have been changed to ensure anonymity.

Dedication

This book is dedicated to my late husband, David William Sohn, who was my soulmate, my playmate, and my teacher. Without the expansive vision, courage, and love of this great man, this powerful work and this book would not exist.

Contents

Foreword

As both founder and director of The Foster Care Institute, and as a foster parent myself to over sixty children who have come through my home and been a part of my family, I have seen up close and personal how anxiety affects children. So many children who experienced trauma were filled with angst. Not only did they suffer emotionally, but their bodies were also often wracked with pain. As a foster parent, at times it was difficult helping these children find the healing they needed.

To be sure, there have been times when I have been filled with anxiety, as well. As I write this, I can recall very clearly the times when my own body was wracked with anxiety and stress. There have been those times when I, too, was crying out for help. Help and relief.

Kathi Sohn notes in chapter one that sometimes we are filled with anxiety when we believe that something out of our control is indeed our fault. I quickly related to this. If you have watched my TED Talk, "Children in Need, Children Ignored," then you know of a story when a foster child living in our home was removed, placed in a stranger's home, raped, and then abandoned. It was not until many years later that we were able to locate her, in a different state and in a mental health hospital. For some time, I felt it was my fault, that I could have done something differently. I could have prevented it somehow. I was riddled with guilt and despair for quite some time.

To say that I was filled with anxiety would be quite an understatement. It took me several years to find peace and healing from it.

Indeed, all of us have faced anxiety in our lives in some way. It reminds me of the saying, "You are either going into the storm, you are in the storm, or you are coming out of the storm."

Many of the biological parents of the children from foster care placed in my home and with my family still suffer from the abuse, neglect, trauma, and anxiety they experienced in their childhood, and never received the professional help, therapy, and counseling they needed.

Yes, we are all going through storms in our lives. Each of us has experienced loss, pain, and anxiety in the past. Tragically, like those parents of the children that I have cared for, many will never find the help that they need.

Indeed, we are experiencing a pandemic of mental health today. According to a study by the Centers for Disease Control (CDC) on mental health issues of teenagers during Covid, more than a third of teens experienced poor mental health during the pandemic. Along with this, just under half, 44 percent of teens said they felt persistently sad or hopeless during the same time period.

When a person experiences trauma and anxiety, it not only affects us mentally, but also affects us physically. I can recall many moments in my life when I felt completely worn down and experienced great fatigue throughout my body. There were mornings when I had a very difficult time "getting going," so to speak, due to the levels of anxiety and pain I felt and experienced.

Perhaps you are in the midst of a storm in your life right now. I am thankful that you have this book in your hands. This book is a much needed one in our society today, and I am grateful to Kathi Sohn for writing it. The tools that Kathi introduces in this book are ones that each of us can use throughout our lives. The Body Memory Process is one tool that I wish I knew about sooner. It is one that I will now teach to the children in my life. Kathi reminds us that we need to be aware of our beliefs, our thoughts, and our words, as they all greatly impact us in many ways. Indeed, our words, beliefs, and thoughts are all powerful tools that can influence us each day, and throughout our lives. Words have power, and so do our thoughts and beliefs. When we begin to recognize and understand this and implement the Body Memory Process, we can then begin to heal.

-Dr. John DeGarmo
Founder/Director of The Foster Care Institute

Introduction

When I was about seven years old, I remember being in the doctor's office, frozen in terror as the white lab coat-clad man sat in his chair waiting for my answer to his question. I just stared at him until my mother broke the silence to respond. The doctor snapped his gaze to her and said, "Ma'am, I asked your *daughter* the question!"

"But she's not answering you!" my mother replied in exasperation.

After that day, I eventually became comfortable talking with individuals, but speaking in or in front of a group of classmates gave me that same feeling of terror I felt in the doctor's office. I know that public speaking is a common fear, but this was gripping dread for just announcing my name! As soon as I knew it was going to be my turn to talk, I would get a huge rush of adrenaline and my heart would start pounding. Once I felt all the attention on me, I would nearly pass out from the overwhelming fear.

When I grew up and needed to speak at work, my problem became more than just an annoyance. It was even further exacerbated when I became a manager. I would look out at the amiable people I engaged with one-on-one every day and see them not as individuals but as an unfriendly, disparaging crowd. The angst I felt was compounded by not wanting to look nervous in front of my employees. My jitters lessened a bit once I joined Toastmasters to get practice speaking in front of a supportive, familiar group. But the problem ultimately persisted, and I would often get bright red blotches on my face and neck when in front of a group I found intimidating.

Then one day, I finally found the solution!

I discovered that my attention anxiety was rooted in the trauma of my earliest days as a rejected, extremely premature baby in intensive care. It was 1961, and I weighed only around two pounds because my birth was the result of an emergency near the end of my distraught birth mother's second trimester. I was peered at very often in my incubator by the medical staff, some either thinking or saying aloud that they didn't believe I would make it. My body might have been tiny and frail, but it still recorded in my body memory the vow, *they watch me to see when I'm going to die.* I'm certain this was also the reason the doctor in the white lab coat frightened me when I was seven.

A powerful, yet not widely known, healing method known as the Body Memory Process helped me discover the root cause of my extreme fear and then taught me how to free myself from it. The result was complete relief from the gripping attention anxiety, and now public speaking is an easy and very fulfilling part of my work.

For more than thirty years, hundreds of other people have had their own breakthroughs using this method and have permanently resolved the issues that it heals. But there are billions of people, and each person has experienced the same phenomenon of creating their core beliefs before they were seven years old, unwittingly carrying those beliefs into adulthood. Unaware that they hold the key, millions of people suffer from a wide range of problems caused by their own belief systems. This is the reason for this book.

According to a March 2022 poll by the American Psychological Association, a large majority of Americans reported high-stress levels associated with the COVID-19 pandemic and its effects, including financial stressors. There is also high concern about global security due to the Russian invasion of Ukraine. Crushing fear over things beyond our control wreaks havoc on our health and ability to function at optimal levels. Add to this the impact of hidden beliefs and the result can be devastating.

There is a very interesting corollary between stress in people and stress in the mechanics of materials. When a metal is subjected to a force it becomes distorted, and the degree of force determines the degree of stress on the metal or internal resistance to try and keep its atoms in their original position. When a person is subjected to a stressor, there is also an internal resistance designed to maintain the status quo because that is safe and known. The problem is that change is constant. Anxiety and fear will have no bearing on the stressor but will cause harm to the physical and mental health of the individual.

Extreme responses to hopelessness and anxiety such as suicides, addiction, and violence against others has dramatically increased since pre-pandemic times. For individual health and societal stability, it is extremely important that people turn inward to explore the reasons they respond the way they do to what is in their environment. There are many opportunities to begin this exploration, including meditation, journaling, and talking with someone who will non-judgmentally listen and reflect what they hear as clues to core beliefs and expectations.

One very powerful way to discover the underlying beliefs that help create stress in our lives is the Body Memory Process, which this book is about.

I am sharing my deep knowledge and experience of the Body Memory Process and its healing of others because I was married to its creator, David William Sohn, for twenty-five years. David passed away in late 2019, leaving behind several gifts which you will learn about in this book.

When I met him in 1994, David was just beginning to write a book on the Body Memory Process at the urging of many clients. It was a slow process because David would leave town on long trips to work with people in other cities and I could only edit when I wasn't at my full-time job with the U.S. Defense Department. During those years, I learned much about the work and had many long conversations with David about our potential to heal anything once we learned to listen to our body. I also did the work needed to heal my intense fear of speaking in front of groups. In 2004, we published the first book on the Body Memory Process, *Escaping the Labyrinth*.

Besides the editing work, I apprenticed with David, sitting in on client sessions and assisting with follow-up coaching. I quickly grew to love the work because I had been fascinated by medicine and wellness since long before meeting David. My earliest advanced studies culminated in an associate's degree in nursing, although by the time I finished the degree I had moved into a career with the federal government. One of my graduate degrees was in conflict analysis and resolution, and David and I had several discussions regarding the applicability of what he discovered within the microcosm of the individual to the macrocosm of interpersonal relations. As an example, just as healing requires an understanding of the root causes of illness, so a peaceful resolution of struggle requires an examination of the underlying breakdown of communication between the parties in conflict. Another example is health is much more than the absence of disease, just as peace is not simply the lack of struggle.

With this book, you will be able to explore what that pain in your shoulders means or why you experience the tightening, burning, headache-causing pain that occurs every time your boss yells at you and you must just stand there and take it.

What if it is not a coincidence? What if it really means something regarding how you have decided to live life? What if somebody yelled at you when you were two or three, after which you decided to not allow it to happen when you were grown? Could it be that the pain in your lower back really does have something to do with your concerns about your job or financial situation? What if it were possible to understand what your body is trying to tell you?

In this book, set up in three parts, you will find the answers to many of the deep mysteries in your life. The first part will lead you through the basics of how and why we create our core beliefs very early in life. Children are naturally sensitive and tuned in to the energies that surround them during their first seven years when they are figuring out how to survive in the world. The scientifically proven mind-body connection provides a means for children to integrate what they learn in a way that assures its application to their future behavior. The problem arises when what the child decided is not logical or does not serve the adult. Humans create their world through thought, language, and belief, and a thorough review of the wisdom on this topic through the ages leads up to an in-depth examination of what is called the *childhood vow*—where thought and emotion join to create a vow, or powerful statement of commitment to an act or condition. My example, *they watch me to see when I'm going to die*, was a vow that declared me as always subject to the scrutiny and judgment of others.

In the second part, you will learn how to discover your own childhood vows by first taking an honest inventory of what is in your life. You will then discover clues to your vows contained within the answers your family can provide and by learning how to listen to your body talk.

The Body Memory Process Body Map will be introduced as a powerful tool to assist with finding your own vows. Over the years of working with hundreds of clients, David noticed patterns emerge—a correlation between his clients' vows and consistent reflection of those vows as pain and tension in certain areas of the body. Other vows would appear in multiple areas, depending upon the impact of that vow on the client's life. For example, finances are very much about security and thus vows related to finances could be reflected in the root chakra area of the body. But issues around finances could also have a big impact on personal power, and thus could reflect in the power chakra area of the body. Massage therapists might notice this too, as when they are massaging a certain sore area they are activating the body memory and the client might start talking about the same issue every time that area is massaged.

In the second part of this book, you will learn what is lovingly termed the Body Memory Process "homework" for working with what you learned during your discovery process. It is by doing the homework that you cause the change you want to see in your life, for this process "empties the cup" (of trapped energy) mentally, physically, and spiritually. This work will create the vacuum necessary to allow something new to fill the space that was taken up for so long by your childhood vows.

The third part of the book is dedicated to all the world of possibility that comes with becoming conscious of our thoughts, our words, and our beliefs. With your new knowledge and awareness, you will create what you want now, as an adult. You will have the tools necessary to address any new vows that might make themselves known as you progress through life. You will also be a much more conscious parent now or when that opportunity might arise in the future. And finally, your work on yourself will contribute to creating higher consciousness on the planet and a better world for everyone.

Are you one of the people who has such a high level of stress and anxiety that you feel your life is spiraling out of your control? Do you have aches and pains that you wish would go away or maybe a pattern in your life you've noticed and want to eliminate? Such patterns could be procrastination, a resistance to taking good care of yourself, or a tendency to free yourself of a problem in one form only to have the problem show up again in another form—such as a woman who divorces an alcoholic and then finds herself married to a gambler.

This book will teach you why these types of problems affect everyone and will also give you the tools you need to explore the reasons for your specific issues. You will see charts and illustrations that will help you understand the concepts, and exercises will help you work through your personal journey of self-discovery. You will find here the tools and encouragement needed to eliminate your problem issues and patterns and enable you to create a happy, healthy, loving, prosperous life.

PART I

HOW YOU
MADE IT UP

CHAPTER ONE

Jenny Learns to Listen to Her Body Talk

Living consciously is essential to health, safety, and quality of life. How many times have you read a news story about someone who forgot to turn off a faucet or forgot about something on the stove, with an expensive and sometimes tragic result? Forgetting important things happens because we don't pay attention to the small things. Disease happens because we don't pay attention to the messages from our body that would alert us to an imbalance. Our body also gives us feedback on our eating, water drinking, and sleep and exercise habits, but are we paying attention?

Sometimes we stop listening because of life's many distractions, and mostly, we tune out feedback because what we decided at a very early age has greatly reduced our ability to live truly in the moment and at choice. We walk around as if in a state of hypnosis, living according to some life-limiting decree and not even aware that we are the one who made it up long ago.

Building your awareness begins with learning to listen to your body again. Your body will help you learn what you created because you are holding those decisions within. They show up as tension, numbness, stiffness, pain, and disease—all messages for you. Listen to and act on those messages and you won't need those physical issues any longer. Many people have healed even "irreversible" diseases because they discovered what they decided and released it.

You might not remember your own earliest childhood years, but your body does. You might not recall being in the womb or what happened at your birth, but your body knows that, too. If you learn to listen, your body will tell you exactly what you decided early on about yourself, others, and life. This is very useful because what you decided back then really does matter to what is happening in your life now. Your body's messages can come to you as chronic issues or acute pain from little accidents, and over time you might start to notice a connection between what is happening in your life and what is happening in your body.

When I became increasingly in tune with my body, I started to notice a pattern whenever I took on a new position at work. I would begin by stubbing a toe or jamming an ankle as I moved through my day. Usually, the accidents would become increasingly painful. One time, a frozen jar of broth slid out of the freezer and landed on my foot.

As I contemplated whether I should just use the jar to ice my wound, I remarked out loud, "Geez, I'm really beating up my feet this week!"

Suddenly, my words shifted my awareness to the fact that feet and legs are about moving forward in life. I then recalled that I was taking on a new position and, as was my usual pattern, I was beginning to doubt whether I could truly step up to the challenge. My husband would always remind me that every time I was new at a job, I would do whatever it took to learn the position and quickly become good at it. As soon as I would settle into this realization, the attacks on my feet would stop!

What is the reason I always had self-doubt when taking on a new assignment? It wasn't about the assignments. Having always stepped up to the challenge in every previous new job didn't matter; there was something in my subconscious that would nag at me, and my body delivered the message every time. I desired to eliminate this pattern for the sake of my feet, and through the self-discovery method discussed in this book,

I learned that the pattern stemmed from my earliest time in the womb when my birth mother had a torrent of self-doubts about becoming a mother. You will see more about patterns and their cause later in the book.

In this chapter, you will meet "Jenny," a Body Memory Process client whose name was changed for anonymity but whose case is real, with all the recorded facts about womb and birth circumstances, difficulties that were showing up in her life, vows that were discovered, and how her life changed after the Body Memory Process session and homework. Other case studies you will read in Part I also contain all these elements. While you read about Jenny's case you will begin learning how childhood vows are imprinted from as early as the womb and discover along with Jenny how your body is always talking to you and listening to your thoughts and emotions. Understanding the way your body and your brain communicate and recognizing how the body sends messages within its systems and to you is key to understanding how childhood vows are formed, sustained, and can ultimately be released.

Since in this chapter you will begin seeing examples of what are termed "vows," I will explain here what a vow is, and you will continue to learn about vows throughout the book.

Have you ever seen the movie *Gone with the Wind*? If so, you will probably recall the powerful scene just before intermission where the character Scarlett O'Hara holds up her fist and emotionally declares, "As God is my witness, I will never be hungry again!"

This is a good example of the wording of a vow (without the ultra-dramatic "As God is my witness" part) and a good demonstration of a strong emotion that accompanies vow creation.

A vow is a promise that is made to oneself about how one will or won't be in the world, and it is formed to be life-affirming. When we are very young, we are trying to figure out how to have our needs met in this world, and being loved is a predominant motivation. Many vows state what we will not tolerate when we are grown, so in keeping them, the individual "chooses" to not have a particular situation in his life. Most vows, however, create non-working behavior patterns, and it is the distress after finally noticing the pattern that drives the person to seek to eliminate the problem.

My vow, *they watch me to see when I'm going to die*, created a non-working pattern in my life that threatened my career and my health. You will see next how Jenny's vows, including *I am helpless* and *I want to die*, were ruining and threatening her life.

Jenny's Story

Jenny sat on her front porch swing one evening, the way she always did at sunset. Watching the sun slip below the horizon usually soothed her, but it seemed that nothing could decrease the agitation she had been feeling all day. Sighing, Jenny leaned back and relaxed into a gentle rocking motion as her thoughts wandered back to her latest failed suicide attempt. She really didn't want to die, but something had to change. Her life was a series of failed relationships, failed pregnancies, and a sense that every time she tried to do something of value for herself it was an inconvenience to others. Jenny had awakened that morning with a feeling of dread that she was caught in a loop from which there was no escape, and the feeling had stayed with her all day.

The rocking of the swing had just put her into a light sleep when she was awakened by her nearby phone. That phone call was the beginning of a healing journey that would forever change her life. It was her boyfriend, Luke, telling her how his brother was very excited about something called the Body Memory Process, which had helped him quickly get to the root cause of some bothersome issues. "Jenny, I think you should do this," Luke almost shouted into the phone. "I'm tired of you never having the spine to make up your own mind about anything."

Taken aback, Jenny quickly asked him if he planned to do a session too, but he immediately changed the subject. Jenny was intrigued and figured she didn't have anything to lose since her life had already hit rock bottom.

When Jenny talked to her mother, Rachel, about wanting to do a session, her mother was relieved that Jenny was taking a positive step and requested to accompany her. As she awaited the session date, Jenny found herself a bit nervous about what she might learn that would reinforce her idea of herself as a failure.

The session started with Jenny first explaining what was in her life now that she wanted to change. "I am hesitant about everything! I never feel truly in charge of my life and whenever I try and make a decision, I immediately think about who it is going to inconvenience. I even stopped trying to commit suicide because I thought it would be too traumatic for someone who discovered me! But I still think I am worthless and although I don't really want to die, I think everything would be better if I were gone." Jenny then explained that her suicide attempts were mainly to get attention.

When it came time for us to explore the earliest memories and experiences of Jenny's life, it was very beneficial that Jenny's mother had joined us. Jenny was quiet while she settled in to learn from Rachel the details of her pregnancy. Jenny had already heard some of the information that came up, but a lot was new and shocking.

Rachel had to quit college for the birth of one daughter and, after going back to school, became pregnant with Jenny and had to quit college again. Jenny's father wouldn't let her mother get an abortion, telling her that if she did, he would divorce her and ruin her life. What was shocking for Jenny is when Rachel admitted that she had the thought, "If you would just die, that would solve my problem."

Jenny had finally discovered the reason she felt she inconvenienced others and why she thought everything would be better if she took her life.

As the session went on and we discovered eleven childhood vows, Jenny became increasingly intrigued by the way her life mirrored what had happened to her mother. She began asking questions about how it all happens and why most people are not in tune with the underlying causes of the problems they experience.

I began to explain, "Our body reflects our subconscious and can give us so much valuable information. The body is always talking to us, but we are taught early in life to ignore what it tells us. Think about what happens when we are very young and fall and scrape a knee. A well-meaning caregiver says, "Oh, it's not that bad—why are you crying? It's just a little scrape!"

Many of us are members of the 'clean plate club' because we were told to eat everything on our plate, even if we weren't hungry anymore. Over time we learned to tune out our body's signals because we were told, often indirectly, that they weren't important."

Jenny started laughing and said, "I'm suddenly finding it funny that I have to set an alarm on my watch to remember to drink water."

We all laughed, then I told Jenny about all the other body signals we ignore. "Your body always tells you when you need to drink water, eat, stop eating, use the bathroom, sleep, move, and stretch. Yes, we need to set an alarm on our watch to drink water because we are too busy during the day to tune in to our body's thirst signals."

I continued, "School and work agendas dictate that we eat on schedule instead of on-demand when we feel our body's hunger cues. At home, we often eat in front of entertainment, so we aren't really enjoying and engaging with our food and our body. We also eat too fast to allow the time needed for the body to send the message that we are full. Work and school schedules also have us using the bathroom only at certain times instead of on-demand when we feel the signal. Social media lures us to ignore cues that it is time to go to sleep, and the internet also helps us ignore messages from our body that it's time to move and stretch."

"Wow, that's fascinating and so true!" Jenny said, then admitted that she was often guilty of staying up way too late watching Tik Tok videos.

Rachel piped up, "Okay, so as adults we have lost our ability to listen to our body, but what role did Jenny's body play in her ending up suicidal because of what I was thinking when I was pregnant with her?"

I explained that:

> Researchers found in the 1970s and 1980s that neurohormonal loops
> link the mother to the unborn child, as glandular substances such as

adrenaline, noradrenaline, serotonin, and oxytocin cross the placenta and can affect the baby. Dr. Thomas Verny, who wrote *The Secret Life of the Unborn Child*, discusses in his book how everything that affects the pregnant mother affects the baby. He found the support of the father during this time to be especially important to the mother, and thus to the baby. Your husband's threat of divorce and abandonment weighed heavily on you and thus deeply impacted Jenny.

If you think about it, as humans we are very connected through our emotions. Think of a time you watched a movie that you thought was especially good and you will realize this was because the creators did a good job of tugging on your emotions and taking you through a range of them throughout the course of the movie. You laughed, you cried, and you felt what the actors portrayed as the emotions of the characters. It wasn't you; it was the character falling in love, dealing with danger, or dealing with a misunderstanding that threatened an important relationship. But it *felt* like it was you because your emotions were activated by what you saw and heard. In much the same way, our emotions become involved in interactions with our parents or primary caregivers, our siblings, and other family members in our earliest years. Only this isn't a movie, and you are involved in real relationships where the strongest emotional bonds are involved.

Another researcher, Dr. Candace Pert, proved that the mind and the body are deeply interconnected. Her research indicated that emotions are conveyed through informational substances like hormones and neuropeptides and are not purely a product of the mind. When a person experiences an emotion, that information is met by biochemical receptors in the body, and this was scientific proof that there is no mind-body barrier. Dr. Pert shifted understanding of the body away from a mechanistic to an informational model.

Jenny's session wrapped up with her receiving the list of vows that we discovered during the discussion and instructions for her homework.

Some clients discover vows by zoning in on where they carry tension, pain, stiffness, numbness, and even disease. For Jenny, her vows were largely linked to time in the womb and showed up most dramatically as her multiple suicide attempts.

Jenny's Vows

The following is a table listing Jenny's eleven vows, when they were created, and how they showed up in her life:

VOW	WHEN FORMED/CAUSE	HOW SHOWED UP FOR JENNY
It's all my fault	Birth	Always felt she was to blame when something was wrong
It's always the wrong time for me	Birth	Difficulty with right timing for decisions
He hurt me	Typical birth thought from predominantly male doctors spanking, poking the newborn	Multiple failed relationships
I am helpless	Birth (mother's thought because of Dad's ultimatum)	Felt helpless in her repeat pattern of suicide attempts and failed relationships
I am too little	Birth	Was told she was "too little" by family growing up
When I get big nobody will do this to me again	Birth	Thought being big would make her better at being in charge, but she was always little, so this contributed to her not feeling in charge
I want to die	Womb (Mom's thought "If you would just die, that would solve my problem")	Would make repeat attention-seeking suicide attempts
I don't know what to do	Womb (mother confused because of Dad's ultimatum)	Often confused when time to make a decision
Men always tell me what to do	Womb (mother's thought because she wasn't allowed to make her own decision)	Always deferred to a man in any major decision
I will be alone	Womb (because of Dad's threat of divorce)	Expected she would end up alone and therefore would always run off her boyfriends

Jenny's Vow Combinations

Vows are very powerful alone and can be especially powerful in combination. Jenny's vow combinations showed up as follows:

1. Combine *I will be alone* with *men always tell me what to do* and her life goes "stale" when she is not in a relationship.

2. Combine *men always tell me what to do* and *when I get big nobody will ever do this to me again* and *I am helpless,* and it explains Jenny never feeling in control in relationships.

3. Combine *it's all my fault* and *I want to die,* and it explains Jenny's suicide attempts.

Results in Jenny's Life after the Body Memory Process Session and Homework Completion

About a year later, Jenny and I met again because she had recommended me to a friend. She hugged me and asked if I wanted to hear a big joke. She had originally worked a session because her boyfriend at the time had told her to, stating that he was sick and tired of her not having a spine and never making up her own mind about anything. After completing her homework, Jenny began making decisions for herself and one of the first ones was to ask her boyfriend to leave because he was so abusive and bossy! Jenny reported that she was taking classes at night school to finish her degree. She had quit college because her boyfriend at the time said it was a "stupid waste of time and that I should get a job." She also reported that her doctor agreed to take her off anti-depressants as a test, so she had not been taking them for about five months. Jenny said, "For the first time in my life I like my body; it is not too little or too big."

Summary of What Jenny Learned About the Wisdom of the Body

1. We listened to our bodies when we were very young, but over time became conditioned that other things and the opinions of others were more important, so we stopped listening.

2. Your body always gives you cues as to when you are hungry, full, thirsty, tired, need the bathroom, and need to move or stretch. It also gives you feedback on your eating, water drinking, and sleep and exercise habits. When you begin paying attention to your body's basic signals for body care you will start to notice other signals, as well. For example, when I cut way back on eating sugar and then had a day when I ate sugar the way I used to, I didn't sleep well because I was very restless. I know it was a message from my body about my choices that day.

3. Your body is always communicating within itself and is an "information system," as termed by neuroscientist Dr. Candace Pert. Your body carries and stores information about your emotions, thoughts, and beliefs.

4. As humans, we are very connected to each other through shared emotions, and this is instrumental in the formation of childhood vows.

5. Your body is always talking to you about what you need to pay attention to in your current life, related to not only your health but also your career, your relationships, and your finances.

Useful Exercises for Integrating What You Learned in This Chapter

1. Take a week to keep a journal on hand to record when you feel thirsty, hungry, full, in need of a stretch, or the first indication that you need to find a bathroom. Also, note what is in your life to regulate when you drink, eat, how fast you need to eat, when you can use the bathroom, and how much time you get to exercise during the day.

2. Think about the last time you hurt yourself and then try to remember what was going on in your life at the time. Can you discover the message from your body? For example, if you hit your head, it could have been a message to not let your brain chatter on and on about something.

3. Tune in to how your body feels when you are relaxed and how it feels when you are stressed and write it in your journal. What do you feel in your body when you are happy? Sad? Confused? Note your feelings and specify where in your body they occur. This exercise will help you get ready to tune in to your body to help discover your childhood vows later in the book.

CHAPTER TWO

Frank Discovers That Children Create Core Beliefs by Age Seven

I must have been ten or eleven years old when I watched a TV commercial that shocked me. It was about minority rights and showed a baby girl wearing a mortar board. The narrator spoke of the girl's right to a 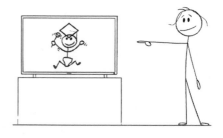 quality education, including the opportunity to go to college. I remember thinking to myself, "Of course!" before I went to find my mother to talk about it.

Mom explained that women were considered a minority in society—an idea that was foreign to me since I had never been taught that at home. I never entertained the idea that I had fewer opportunities than men, and I faced no problems getting access to quality education or advancement at work. One could say this was because of federal civil rights laws. However, if I had been told before the age of seven that I would have to struggle for many things because I was female, my experience might have been different.

Children don't just gradually learn about the world as they progress through the K-12 program, finally ready for adulthood at age seventeen or eighteen. By the time they are in second grade, they have already largely determined how they are, how others are, and how life is.

Examples are: *I am a disappointment, they never tell me the truth,* and *life is hard.* Children create their core beliefs and childhood vows through interactions with mainly parents or other primary caregivers. They are also influenced during their early years by siblings, other relatives they may see frequently, babysitters, teachers, and daycare providers.

Kids will learn facts about the world and the opinions of others as they progress through school, but by the time they are seven years old, they have assembled their childhood vows into a "survival kit" for life. The child is subconsciously motivated to form vows to survive in the world, but childhood vows are far from true survival mechanisms and can even be life-threatening to the adult.

My two brothers and I were each adopted after especially traumatic beginnings that involved the loss of our natural parents. My brother Gary was already three years old by the time he was adopted. By then he had lived in several foster homes and must have been so afraid of further rejection that he stiffened up whenever he was hugged. I remember my mother telling me that Gary only reciprocated a hug once when he was very ill. As Gary grew up, the pattern of rejection he created before he was three became gradually apparent, and by the time he was an adult, it was blazingly clear. He was constantly kicked out of schools for his behavior until there was no place left that he could attend locally. When he went to a boarding school for troubled youth, he was put on Ritalin and barely recognized his family when we visited.

Gary ran away from home when he was seventeen, had a very brief marriage that lasted about six months, then had a baby out of wedlock who he wasn't allowed to visit. He joined the Army but was dishonorably discharged within the first year and spent the rest of his life traveling around the country doing odd jobs or sitting in jail because of drug use or criminal behavior that he'd been lured into. One of Gary's odd jobs must have involved exposure to asbestos, because he died in his forties from mesothelioma.

Thankfully, in recent years there has been an effort to educate all those who work with disturbed children on the need for "trauma-informed care," reducing the previous tendency to simply dismiss a traumatized child with behavior issues as a problem for someone else to solve.

I never had the opportunity to help Gary, but if I had, I am sure we would have discovered childhood vows that were formed before he was three that created for him continual rejection as a self-fulfilling prophecy. I would expect vows such as *nobody wants me, I'm not good enough*, or *it's all my fault*.

In this chapter, you will meet Frank, a Body Memory Process client who, like Jenny, became dissatisfied with a life pattern and decided to do something about it. While you read about Frank's case to learn how childhood vows impacted his life, you will learn how and why children form childhood vows.

Frank's Story

Frank sat in the traffic jam staring at the license tag on the car in front of him. It read "LAZEE1" and he couldn't help thinking it was a message  for him. Frank knew he was in a rut, and it worried him that the health article he had recently read might be true.

The article opened with, "Do you think of yourself as a couch potato?" and then went on to explain the health risks associated with a sedentary lifestyle. Frank indeed thought of himself as a lazy person—coming home from work every day to flip on the television to help him forget the typical lousy day at work.

Today was an especially annoying day when the boss, Mr. Hill, called an impromptu meeting to discuss an office policy violation. Someone was using the office Xerox machine to photocopy huge personal documents, using reams of office paper, and going through expensive ink cartridges. Mr. Hill didn't know who it was because he spent most of his time in his private office. But he figured someone who worked out on the floor must know.

As Frank sat tapping his fingers on the steering wheel, he reviewed the meeting in his mind. At one point, Mr. Hill had looked right at him and said, "Frank—do you know who's been doing this?"

Caught off guard, Frank had managed to stammer, "I—I don't know. It wasn't me!"

"I didn't say I thought it was you, Frank. But since your desk is close to the printer, you should have noticed someone spending a lot of time photocopying."

"No, I didn't see anything! Maybe John saw something—his desk is close to the printer, too!"

John shot Frank a look of disbelief that he was trying to deflect heat from the boss onto him. Frank felt his own incredulity that he had just done that, although it wasn't the first time that he had quickly "passed the buck" when questioned about his involvement in or knowledge of an issue at work.

Frank was tired of the traffic jam and of staring at the license tag, so he ducked off at the next exit to visit a coffee shop for a cappuccino. Standing in line, his eye caught a flyer announcing a free one-hour introduction to the Body Memory Process that coming Friday. "Come learn how childhood vows could be running and ruining your life now" grabbed his attention at a time when he was feeling particularly fed up with his confusing behavior pattern, and he decided to attend the event.

Frank sat in the audience waiting for the presentation to begin, thinking it was probably going to be a waste of time, and then a little over an hour later found himself standing in line waiting to sign up for a session.

The following Wednesday evening, Frank was talking about his father. "In my house, you had better not give the wrong answer to my father or there would be a lot of yelling! After a particularly long rant one evening when I was about six, my brothers took me aside and said the best thing to do is just say 'I don't know' if I wasn't sure of the right answer. Dad could accept that a lot better. After that night, I started paying more attention to how other family members answered Dad, and I even noticed my mother saying 'I don't know' a lot. It's interesting that through the years there have been times I thought I should know an answer that I just can't remember."

"Frank, it's early in your session, but I think you are already on to one of your childhood vows—*I don't know*. Your brothers advised you to say "I don't know" as a survival mechanism around your raging father, and you grabbed onto it like a lifeline."

Frank replied, "Yes, I hate being yelled at!"

"How was your relationship with your mother?"

Frank laughed and said it was good, adding, "I think both she and Dad were trying for a girl when they had me since they already had two boys. I remember my mother always calling me "Sweetie Boy" until I was about nine when she finally had my sister!"

Frank then looked thoughtful for a moment before asking me to explain the creation of vows. "I was intrigued by your presentation last Friday and would like to learn more about how little kids make decisions about themselves. I studied psychology in college and really enjoyed the course."

"Do you recall studying *child* psychology?" I asked.

"Yes, a little, but please give me a quick refresher because it's been a while!"

I began, "Many major theories of child development stress the importance of a child's interaction with primary caregivers during the earliest years. The most accepted theory of emotional development is Eric Erikson's psychosocial theory, placing the key to emotional health during the period of birth to eighteen months when the baby is determining whether they can trust the people around them to meet their needs."

Frank spoke up, "I remember studying Erikson now! Didn't he say that mistrust can occur before the age of two, and then during the next two stages the child can experience shame, doubt, and guilt?

"That's right, and did you also study John Bowlby's attachment theory?

Bowlby's work was very important to understanding emotional and social development, identifying the role of the caregiver as critical to a child's sense of safety and security and to the regulation of negative emotions. Like the role of trust early on, the ability of a child to form secure attachments with caregivers is foundational to their future ability to form healthy emotional bonds in life.

"Then there is Jean Piaget's theory of cognitive development, which is also relevant to the formation of childhood vows. According to Piaget, children are not logical and are also very ego-centric until the age of seven. Add this to the fact that young children are always immersed in the potential to perceive or misperceive a reason to mistrust, feel shame, doubt, or guilt and you can see how emotionally-driven beliefs—often about themselves—can form."

Frank asked, "What about young children and their imaginations? Does that play a role?"

"Yes, indeed it does! If you haven't already heard Dr. Bruce Lipton talk about children from time in the womb until age seven being in the theta brain wave state of imagination, I recommend pulling up one of his educational videos or reading *The Biology of Belief*. Dr. Lipton lectures on how the first seven years of life determine your future, and that the subconscious mind contains our programming and our habits that were formed during these years. Many result from negative emotional experiences."

Frank asked, "Can childhood vows be formed out of positive emotional experiences?"

"That is an excellent question and yes, absolutely! Consider this scenario. I am three years old and I don't get a lot of attention from my very busy daddy who is away a lot for work. One day, I am sitting on his knee and have his undivided attention. At one point he looks at me and says, 'Don't forget you will always be my little girl!' Remember, at this age I'm not logical and I'm the center of my universe. So, during this very happy time, I file away what will assure my beloved daddy's attention. *I will always be your little girl.*

"The difficulty arises when I'm thirty-five years old and a powerful male in my life (such as my boss) activates this vow, and in his presence I seem to transition from being a mature woman to a giggling little girl. Most importantly, I suddenly *feel* like a little girl, unsure of myself and disempowered in the presence of authority. Other people around me can see it, but I am unaware that this decision I made when I was three is impacting my feelings and my behavior."

Frank gave a big sigh and said, "I can understand the joy of getting your daddy's undivided attention. I remember when I was young thinking nobody really cared about me. My parents were very busy and out of the house a lot. My brothers were both older and didn't like me hanging around them too much. I still don't think people really care about me unless they give me their undivided attention."

"Some childhood vows you need to search for. Some just jump right out at you when you start talking about your childhood and then take a look at what is still true for you now. Frank, I would say another one of your vows is *they don't care about me*. What else concerns you in your life right now?"

Frank gave a huge sigh then said with a wry smile, "How much time did you say you had? I am often disgusted with myself at work. I am so afraid of derision from the boss that I am quick to pass the buck and end up being disdained by my colleagues. I feel like I can't win!"

"Okay, Frank," I said. "Let's go back to a scenario from your childhood when your father would get angry with you. How did you deal with it?"

"I remember wanting to get my father's attention off me and would sometimes tell him that my brothers had said it was okay to do what my father was upset about. This would work a lot of times because my father would storm off to find my brothers."

"We often make vows to deal with situations such as yours with your father, then find those vows activated when we are in a relationship with a powerful male in your life. Such a vow activation is an opportunity to discover and deal with this childhood artifact."

"It's not just at work that I feel like a failure," said Frank. "I think every morning that this is the day I'm going to start exercising after I get home from work. But after sitting in traffic and thinking about my lousy day, I can't wait to just turn on the television or the internet and forget about my life. I am the epitome of the lazy couch potato."

Suddenly, Frank sat up straight and said, "Oh, my God! I just remembered something! My father used to tell me I was lazy because he'd often find me on the couch reading a book instead of playing sports after school. It wasn't that I didn't like being outside playing, I just liked reading! Wait, let me guess, I have a vow *I am lazy!*"

Frank continued excitedly, " That must be one of my vows! I remember hearing the disappointment in Dad's voice when he said how much he wished I was more athletic." His voice lowered a bit as he added, "It made me feel very sad that I was such a failure in his eyes."

I gently said, "It was that emotional, defining moment that led you to accept your dad's evaluation of you as lazy and you took it as your own belief."

Once again energized by his own realization of the vow, *I am lazy,* Frank stood up from the couch. "I've got to get more active! I've been worried about my health because I developed childhood-onset diabetes when I was a kid and have been on insulin ever since. I don't want any more issues."

As soon as Frank said this, I recalled him saying that his mother called him "Sweetie" for years.

"Frank, have you ever read Louise Hay's book *You Can Heal Your Life* or Deb Shapiro's *Your Body Speaks Your Mind?* If you look up these books, you will see they have discovered that children can develop diabetes after either feeling they are a cause of parental conflict or due to a smothering and excessively indulgent parent. You said your mother would call you 'Sweetie' a lot. How did you feel about that?"

Frank said his mother was out of the house a lot but when she was home, she tried to make up for it by calling him 'Sweetie' and treating him like a baby. When I suggested he might have given in to this because he loved her, Frank agreed and we determined the likely wording of the vow as *I'll be your sweet baby.*

I took the opportunity to explain to Frank that there is no such thing as a "good vow" and that any vow that is operating subconsciously takes away conscious choice in any moment. Being his mom's sweet baby might not seem like such a bad thing, but it had been taking a toll on his body. Think of the vow *I'll always be happy*. That sounds like a great vow to have! But what about when you aren't happy? Sometimes it is important to mourn the loss of someone or be in another state of mind to fully experience life.

Frank's session wrapped up with a list of eight vows and instructions for homework. Frank had one vow that manifested as a physical disease and the others showed up as nuisances in his work and social life.

Frank's Vows

The following is a table summarizing Frank's eight vows, when they were created, and how they showed up in his life. Frank's vow, *I don't know*, is what is termed a "family jewel," handed down from one generation to the next, just like the family jewels. Sometimes parents consciously say a statement that they don't realize is a vow, just a sort of motto about the family, such as "The Smiths are hard workers," or "The Joneses are God-fearing people." These very powerful vows are the building blocks of work ethic, prejudices, religious belief, ethnic behavior, and a host of other societal patterns.

The vow *I don't know* was a way for Frank's family to cope with a husband and father who was prone to rage, and there is a good chance this could be passed along to any grandchildren. It also could have been passed on from previous generations if rage was a family pattern.

VOW	WHEN FORMED/CAUSE	HOW SHOWED UP FOR FRANK
I don't know	Child—family jewel	Frank had much confusion in life and often found himself feeling like he should know an answer that he just couldn't remember
They don't care about me	Infant/child (always felt left out); brothers didn't want him around; parents not around much	Frank never believed anyone cared about him unless he had their undivided attention—which caused him to appear very needy
I am lazy	Child (was told he was lazy because he was a book-worm, not an athlete)	Frank claimed to be a "couch potato," which he didn't like
If they see me, they won't like me	Birth (parents said throughout pregnancy they hoped it would be a girl)	Frank didn't like meeting new people and always had to "look right;" he never liked for anyone to just drop in when he wasn't prepared
I'll be your sweet baby	Infant/Child (Mom would call him "my sweet baby" and "my sweet boy" until his sister was born when he was nine years old)	Childhood onset diabetes
Life is a struggle	Birth	Frank struggled with his health and at work
I'd better keep my mouth shut	Child (Another strategy besides saying "I don't know" was to be quiet when Dad raged)	This was how he mainly interacted with dominant males at work, and it caused a lot of difficulties
I am not the one you want	Child (Often convinced father he wasn't the guilty one to avoid trouble)	Frank always tried to pass the buck even when he wasn't suspected to be at fault

Frank's Vow Combinations

Vows are very powerful alone and can be especially powerful in combination. Frank's vow combination showed up as follows:

> Combine *They don't care about me* and *I am not the one you want* with *If they see me they won't like me* to create a strong pattern of hiding in any relationship.

Results in Frank's Life After the Body Memory Process Session and Homework Completion

Frank stopped taking insulin a year after starting the work on himself because he was able to control his blood sugar with a change of diet, activity, and thought. Frank moved to live in the mountains and took up hiking. He realized he liked the outdoors so much that he changed his career to one that allowed him to be outdoors a lot. Frank laughed when he said, "I didn't know an MBA could get a job in the woods!"

Frank's new job also involved a lot more responsibility and he was finally in a serious relationship.

Summary of What Frank Learned About the Creation of Childhood Vows Before Age Seven

1.   By the time children are seven years old, they have assembled their childhood vows into a "survival kit" for life. The child is motivated to form a vow to survive in the world, but childhood vows are far from true survival mechanisms and can even be life-threatening to the adult.

2.   Before the age of seven, children are not logical, are very egocentric, and are immersed in the potential to perceive (or misperceive) a reason to mistrust, feel shame, have doubts about their security, and feel guilt that something is all their fault.

3.   During the first seven years of life, children are in the theta brain wave state, which is like a state of hypnosis, when they are learning the programs and habits that will guide their future. Children will often witness and have negative emotional experiences during this time, which will influence the creation of childhood vows.

4.   Vows can also form during positive emotional events, and these vows can create difficulties for the adult as much as negative emotional events.

5. Vows can come in the form of "family jewels," passed from one generation to the next.

6. There is no such thing as a "good vow" because any vow that is operating subconsciously takes away conscious choice in any moment.

Useful Exercises for Integrating What You Learned in This Chapter

1. Consider the following examples of what could be considered "good vows" and pick one to write a paragraph on the problems such a vow could cause in someone's life. Example "good vows" are:

   a. *Life is easy*

   b. *I am perfect*

   c. *Everyone loves me*

   d. *I love everyone*

2. Choose a traumatic event that a four-year-old could experience and create a list of vows that the child could end up with, along with their cause and how those vows could show up much later in life.

3. Relax and think about your childhood. Is there anything you would observe your mother or father doing regularly? What were your thoughts about what they did? If you can remember any, write them down and then think about anything in your life now that might be the result of those thoughts. For example, I remember watching my mother iron things like underwear and sheets and thinking I would never do that when I grew up! I don't buy materials that wrinkle easily and don't even own an iron!

CHAPTER THREE

Mary Finds Peace in the Dance Between Competence and Change

Chaos is a widely misunderstood concept. Many people will do anything to avoid it because they fear the change it can bring. Some try to control it and end up causing problems for themselves and for others. Defined as randomness, formlessness, unpredictability, and confusion, chaos can cause lots of anxiety because we tend to associate the unknown with danger. Yes, chaos brings change, but what about the joy it could also bring?  An artist staring at a blank canvas, holding his palette of colors, is in chaos until he organizes the beautiful images he wants to convey. Teach your feet and arms the individual steps of a dance and you will feel a very worthwhile chaos until dedicated practice allows you to gracefully become one with the music.

The truth about chaos is that its apparent randomness is but an illusion, its formlessness is full of exciting possibility, and its unpredictability portends the arrival of something fresh and new. In this chapter, you will meet a Body Memory Process client, "Mary," who will learn that childhood vows can be formed and reinforced when caregivers are stuck in their own pattern of trying to manage chaos. Healing from our childhood vows and becoming conscious parents can only occur when we learn to embrace chaos, knowing we are competent to handle the change called healing and every change life will bring.

Parents need to consistently manage their own fears as they engage with growing children and an ever-shifting safety landscape. I am aware that whenever I've needed to allow my children a little more freedom, I've also had to deal with my brain throwing out all the associated dangers. If I let my fears take the lead and don't take the risk of letting go a little, I am attempting to control the chaos by avoiding it. Of course, confronting it is inevitable because children must grow up, learn from their own mistakes, and launch independent lives.

Sometimes we need to deal with unhealed trauma from our own childhood and persistent fears around issues like money. Because of their own persistent traumas, parents can inadvertently facilitate the creation and reinforcement of childhood vows. To illustrate, I'll share a story about an interaction with my daughter, Sarah, which surprised me with the message that I still needed to work on some fear around money.

Ever since she could eat a solid diet, Sarah has liked a wide variety of food, so it always surprises me when she discovers something she *doesn't* like. One day when she was eight years old, I bought her something that was a little expensive but because I was sure she would like it, I thought it would be a fun surprise. As it turns out, Sarah did not like it at all, pushing it away saying, "You can eat it, Mom."

It was too sweet for me, and I felt the anger course through my body as I slammed the container into the garbage saying, "Geez, Sarah! You must think I'm made from money!"

Immediately, my words rang in my ears and I cringed, realizing it is during such interactions that childhood vows can form. I immediately softened, walked around the counter to embrace her, and gently said, *"I'm sorry, I was wrong. I want you to always feel you can express your opinion, and* **your opinion is more important to me than money."**

Here is what could have played out if I didn't put in a correction right away. Sarah's emotionally laden thought (vow) could be, *I won't tell her what I really feel*, or *money is more important than how I feel*, or *money is more important than what I think.*

Fast forward to Sarah's potential future during her teenage years after this belief has been rooted into place and reinforced. During a time when communication between mother and daughter is very important, the vow *I won't tell her what I really feel* could have damaged Sarah's relationship with me and limited my ability to interact with her on a deep, meaningful level. Fast forward to Sarah's potential adult life and the vow *money is more important than how I feel*, or *money is more important than what I think* could inadvertently trap her in a job that pays well but isn't fulfilling—or she could endure an abusive boss because she believes her thoughts and feelings aren't worth expressing.

You will next meet a Body Memory Process client named "Mary" who grew up with a fearful, needy mother and a father with strong expectations that heavily influenced her personality.

Mary's Story

Mary looked at the sky and thought it might start snowing soon. She mentally debated whether she should call her parents and use the impending storm as an excuse to miss Thanksgiving dinner and the fight at the table that was bound to happen. For as long as she could remember, holidays at home were usually painful, not joyful.

"Better get going early," Mary thought.

She decided to brave the weather and the forty-five-mile drive to her parents' house for Thanksgiving dinner rather than the criticism she would receive if she didn't show up. As it turned out, the weather wasn't what she expected. The dinner, however, was. This year, the fight started when Mary's mother asked her why she never invited her to come visit. "What are you hiding, Mary? Is your place always a mess or something?"

Mary had shot back, "No, Mom! It's so clean most of the time you can eat off the floor—unlike this place!"

Everything went down-hill when Mary's mother said she didn't like her tone of voice and then her dad jumped in to tell his wife to leave Mary alone.

Driving back home, Mary let the negative energy she felt at her parents' home wash over her as she reviewed everything in her life that was wrong. She didn't understand her compulsion to constantly clean her body and her home and why she was always so appalled by the messy house her mother had always kept. To her, everything had to be perfect, but her life was far from flawless. She liked men, but didn't like having to make herself look feminine and pretty just to go on a date. She found it hard to make decisions, which often resulted in a fiasco. "I don't know why I try so hard," Mary thought and heaved a sigh. "I can't make a relationship work for more than a few weeks and just I feel like such an all-around failure!"

That evening, Mary was still feeling depressed when she saw a Facebook ad with two ballroom dancers and the words, "Life is a dance between competence and change . . . Stop trying to balance chaos and control."

Feeling like the message was created just for her, Mary went to the referenced website and became interested enough in the Body Memory Process to make an appointment for a discovery session.

Mary showed up for her session about five minutes late and apologized like it had been an hour. When I told her five minutes late was not a big deal, she said it was so for her. "I am never late for anything, and I submit all my work projects on time!"

"How does your body feel when you are occasionally a little late like today?"

"Like someone punched me in the gut."

That's a big clue to a probable childhood vow such as *I am always on time*. As the conversation continued, it became clear it was more about being perfect than specifically being on time.

Mary then began talking about her childhood as a tomboy and said it was no secret that her father really wanted a boy. "I always preferred to hang around my dad when he was working on the car or building something in the garage. I didn't want to do anything that girls usually did with their mom like baking cookies or playing with makeup. I know it's not a good thing to say, but I never really liked being with my mother all that much. According to both my parents, I was their perfect little girl, yet my mother was always picking at me about something, like being too independent or too noisy. I even remember my mother telling me that archaic expression, 'Children should be seen and not heard.' I hadn't thought about that in years! Could that be why I tend to be quiet and have difficulty expressing my feelings?"

I answered, "Yes, children create their core belief system by observing the world around them when they are very young. They are immersed in a very small world with their primary caregivers, the role models who are always with them. If their parents are carrying around their own baggage from early childhood, they are likely to try and control what is in their world. Being run by their own subconscious behavior patterns, parents can say things that help reinforce their children's current vows and inadvertently cause the creation of new ones. Your mother might have been told 'Children should be seen and not heard' when she was a child and then passed it along to you."

"Why do parents try to keep children quiet?" Mary asked as she leaned forward in her seat with her hands clasped around her neck.

I noted that Mary's body language was clearly indicating a vow associated with her communication chakra, *I will be quiet.*

"There are times when it is appropriate to keep children quiet, such as while others are ill, studying, or sleeping. Having a rule that children must stay quiet as possible all the time is an attempt to maintain control in a house. A child obeying a rule to stay quiet can't ask questions that are difficult to answer. Children bring chaos, and by this I'm not talking about their loud talking and nearly constant movement. The chaos that children bring is unpredictability and great potential, but adults can subconsciously resist the imperfect and the incomplete. Life can condition adults to be so goal-focused that they forget to enjoy the journey. More importantly, they can forget the excitement and creativity that came when they first decided they wanted to take that journey. In this way, there can be a huge gap between the natural 'beingness' of children and the conditioned 'doingness' of parents.

"Babies and young children are immersed in the learning process and are therefore always in a state of chaos, adding to and organizing what they already know. They don't get fearful that they don't know something because they aren't yet aware of what they are supposed to learn. They aren't anxious that they are blocked or falling behind because they don't know what the end of the journey is supposed to look like. You can ask a six-year-old what he wants to be when he grows up and the answer will likely change when his class visits the fire station because he is truly living in the moment, not some future when he will be grown. Children are mainly unaware that their minds are constantly expanding and that their bodies are continually growing. Instead of fear, they excitedly anticipate each birthday as a milestone along their journey of continual change."

Mary laughed and said when she last asked her niece what she wanted to be when she grows up, she said she wanted to run the merry-go-round they had just gotten off. Her face quickly changed to a serious expression as she asked if I knew why she constantly needed to clean herself and her house.

"What do you know about your birth?" I asked.

"Not much. I don't think there were any big problems. I know the doctor had to use forceps. Oh, and I was born with something called meco . . . meconi . . . something stain."

"Meconium stain?"

"That's it!"

"First of all, babies born with forceps can have a birth vow, *I can't do it myself . . .*" I hardly had that out when Mary excitedly told me this explained why she found it hard to make a decision without someone telling her what to do.

"People ask me how I can stand having such a micro-managing boss, but I've always liked being told every step to take at work. That way I don't ever have to worry about making a mistake. Uh oh . . . there's that perfectionism again!"

Mary and I laughed and then I addressed her other birth issue. "Meconium stain occurs when some of the nearly born baby's meconium stool gets into the amniotic fluid and can discolor the baby's skin and cause breathing issues. I have had several clients who were meconium stain babies report they seem to never feel clean enough."

Mary blushed a little as she said, "Well, interestingly, I don't like being dirty, but I only seem to like sex that is a little kinky or in a place where we might get caught."

"Many, many people end up with a vow, *sex is bad,* that causes them to have such preferences. It is most often caused by their conception being an accident after passionate, unprotected sex."

"Oh wow, I remember my mother telling me she and dad had to get married because of me and that she was ashamed of being pregnant out of wedlock. I can't believe how much of my issues are about my parents! I also feel sorry for my mom and am wondering if we will ever be able to fix our relationship. It's just every time we are together, we argue, and every time we argue, I want to be the one who ends up in control. I need to either win or be the one to end the argument by storming out of the house."

"Situations won't resolve with control, and very often the solution appears only with the relinquishment of it. Sometimes it takes surrendering to a new way of doing things, and sometimes it takes letting things hit bottom for everyone involved to learn. You came to the Body Memory Process because you want to surrender the patterns that just aren't working in your life. Surrendering what has been comfortable and familiar but which still holds you back from a much more fulfilling, joyful life is the only way to truly heal.

"I remember an exercise in surrender that I participated in many years ago. I needed to sit in a chair and follow the command, 'Palms together, palms apart, palms up, palms down.' During the first fifteen or twenty minutes, my brain kept chattering away. 'Why are we doing this? This is stupid. What does doing these silly hand movements have to do with surrender? I want to stop doing this!' Then finally I felt myself surrender to just following the command.

"I stopped being in my head and let myself feel what was happening in my body. I stopped thinking about the steps and just let them happen automatically, and what I moved into was a feeling that could only be described as bliss."

Mary asked, "But isn't surrendering quitting?"

"Surrender is not quitting. It is a leap of faith to move forward without your brain in charge. When you stop trying to balance chaos and control, you realize life is like a dance between competence and change. In an unchoreographed dance, one partner leads and the other follows. If you are willing to accept that change is inevitable, you can be sure you are best prepared to meet that challenge. Through self-discovery and healing, you will find yourself increasingly capable to meet whatever change comes your way. You will be willing to take more risks to let change take the lead as you then competently respond."

Mary said she was ready to stop the constant washing and wanted to figure out how to have a new relationship with her mom. She also wanted to see what life would be like without needing someone to tell her what to do all the time. Her session wrapped up with a list of fifteen vows and instructions for homework. Most of Mary's vows involved her self-identity and self-esteem, and heavily impacted her family, work, and personal relationships.

Mary's Vows

VOW	WHEN FORMED/CAUSE	HOW SHOWED UP FOR MARY
I am fine	Womb (first-born)	Does like to talk about her feelings
It's all my fault *Sex is bad*	Conception Trauma (mom and dad had to get married and were ashamed)	Adult Mary always felt very guilt-ridden, and sex was bad for her unless it was "dirty" or "kinky"
I will be your boy, Dad	Womb (dad really wanted a boy)	Was a tomboy; puberty and dating process were negative; nicknamed "George"
I will not be like her	Womb (mom and dad fought about mom's neediness and unwillingness to live away from her parent.)	Mary and her mom fought a lot about Mary's independence—while Mary's mom continued strong dependence on Mary's dad
I don't want to be here	Womb (mom's thought)	Mary almost died as an infant
I am dirty	Birth (had meconium stain at birth)	Adult Mary could "never get clean" and was constantly washing
I can't do it by myself	Birth (forceps used during delivery)	Worked well with micro-managing boss; almost always allowed situations to deteriorate due to her indecision
He hurt me	Birth (typical birth thought from predominantly male doctors spanking, poking the newborn)	Relationships usually ended with extreme hurt from betrayal
I will be just like you, Dad	Infant (dad was so happy and mom so unhappy that Mary decided to be like her dad)	Mary was in the same profession as her dad
I will be quiet	Child (was told "children should be seen and not heard" and was told she was a noisy child)	Mary had a problem with self-expression
I am never good enough for them *I will be perfect* *I will make them love me the way I am*	Child (mom and dad always told her she would be a "perfect little girl" and always wanted her to do and be better)	Mary bemoaned the fact she could never give an inch in a relationship where she felt she was judged, and the relationships inevitably failed
There is never enough for me	Infant (Mom had problems breast-feeding and parents struggled financially)	Mary reported life-long problems with being overweight

Mary's Vow Combinations

1. The combination of *I will be your boy, Dad, I will not be like her,* and *I will be just like you, Dad,* created such a strong pattern that Mary was incapable of patterning feminine behavior.

2. Add to the combination in (1) above, the vow *sex is bad,* and Mary found herself incapable of a satisfactory relationship.

3. The combination *I am never good enough for them* and *I will be perfect* made her refer to herself as a "failed perfectionist."

Results in Mary's Life After the Body Memory Process Session and Homework Completion

About eight months after her discovery session, Mary came to a Body Memory Process introductory session and told the group that one of the best things that had happened because of her session and homework was her very reduced tendency to procrastinate—as she had released her need to be perfect. Mary stated that she was in a different job because she had found the ability to stand up for herself. Further, she was picking famous women to read about and decide which of their characteristics she would like to copy in her own life. Mary said she had ended her non-working relationship and was actively looking for a man who would reciprocate true, non-judgmental love.

Summary of What Mary Learned About Chaos, Control, Change, and Competence

1. While protecting their children, parents need to constantly face their own fears (and vows). If they resist and are unaware of their subconscious motivations, they might try to control the chaos and uncertainty. The result can be the formation and reinforcement of their children's vows.

2. Life can condition adults to be so destination-focused that they forget to enjoy the journey and the experience of life. Most children don't know or care about goals. They live in the moment with great excitement and creativity. This can cause a gap between children and their caregivers, resulting in such childhood vows as *nobody understands me* or *something must be wrong with me*. Remember, children are not logical, and they tend to blame themselves. "Nobody" probably just means mom and dad, but to the adult dealing with the vow, it means nobody in the world.

3. You must be willing to surrender control if you want to find the solution to non-working patterns and relationships in your life. Often, people seek help when they realize they are "sick and tired of being sick and tired."

4. Surrender is not quitting. It is a leap of faith to move forward without your brain in charge. It is your brain's job to keep you safe, but it does this with a sort of algorithm based on your past experiences. The truth is your past experiences were the result of your thoughts and beliefs in the past. You have the opportunity now to think and believe differently.

5. We are often told, "control yourself," and that control is the answer to many of life's challenges. A much more empowered approach is to accept the inevitability of change and make yourself as competent as possible through self-awareness and healing.

Useful Exercises for Integrating What You Learned in This Chapter

1. If you are a parent, think about when you needed to decide whether to allow your child to do something new. Pick a time when you felt a little anxious about taking a risk and grappled with the associated dangers. An example is the first time I let my daughter ride along with a friend who was driving a toy

car. I felt myself slip forever from a time when I would not have allowed it into the moment of seeing the joy on her face as they zipped across the parking lot. My impulse had been to say "no!" once again, but I let go of the control. There was still a threshold for all the things I wouldn't yet approve. But there always comes a time to now say "yes" to something—and that's the moment I would like you to remember if you can. Write down how it felt to make the decision and how it felt to watch the results. If you are not a parent, pick a time when you said "yes" to *yourself* for the first time—allowing *yourself* to experience something you were previously scared to do. Write down how it felt to make the decision and how it felt to have the new experience.

2. Remember a tight control one or both of your parents had on you when you were young. What was it that you were sure you were ready and able to do, but were not allowed to do? I asked my parents to build me a chemistry lab and provide me with a bunch of equipment so that I could do experiments. They were probably concerned that I'd blow up the backyard, but I remember being hurt that they didn't think I was smart enough to run a chemistry lab. Did you make any decisions about yourself because of something you weren't allowed to do? Did you make any decisions about your parent/s or about life? Write down whatever you remember and be sure to keep it handy for when you work on discovering a list of your childhood vows.

3. Have some fun and create a surrender challenge for yourself! You could use the "palms up, palms down . . ." exercise I describe in this chapter or create any repetitive movement that you can do for a period (usually about fifteen to twenty minutes). Make a note of what you feel in your body when your brain stops asking you why you are doing what you are doing!

CHAPTER FOUR

Ann Experiences the Power of Words in Thought, Belief, and Vow Creation

It was a typically sunny, gorgeous Hawaiian honeymoon day. My new husband and I were lounging on the sparkling Kauai beach when something untypical happened. I don't remember why,  but that day we had chosen to sit on the beach with our backs to the sea. We carefully looked at where the sand was wet, then let the salty breeze help open our big beach towel into a position well out of reach of the waves—or so we thought. I was just about to pull my book out of my backpack when I heard the loud roar. We both looked around too late to scramble out of the way of the rogue wave that crashed over us, drenching everything.

As we laughed and started wringing out the towel, I suddenly remembered my camera was in the soaking wet backpack. I took it out and shook off the water, my mood sinking as I wondered if my beautiful pictures of the previous two islands could be saved. This was the time before cell phones, and a roll of film did not enjoy the protection that photos do in the digital age.

I ran into the first camera shop we could get to and asked the technician if the wet film could be saved. He looked at me, looked at the film, looked back at me, and said, "I don't know, I'll try . . ."

My husband said it was a blur, I was out the door so fast with the film. The next technician I talked to said, "Yes! I can definitely take care of this for you." He saved all the pictures.

Words are incredibly powerful. They evoke the senses, stir the emotions, instill trust, or cause doubt. They also give you insight into intention. The first camera technician used the word "try," which did not make me confident at all. He could have said this to someone else who might have deemed him courageous for agreeing to make an attempt in the face of uncertainty. For me, the word "try" does not carry the commitment necessary to produce the desired result. If a technician says, "I will try to save your pictures," the intention is on the trying.

If a technician says, "I will save your pictures," the focus is on the doing. As Master Yoda says in Star Wars, "Do or do not, there is no try."

As previously discussed, we create beliefs based on our pre-logical interpretation of the world during our formative years. Discovering the specific wording of these beliefs delivers the absolute, behavior-defining aspects of the vow. This is found in the meaning of the vow, as it limits our life experience. If the words are *I will do it myself*, the vow means "I will accept no help."

Doing something myself is commendable because there is growth and learning involved. The limitation comes in when I refuse to accept help, because everyone needs help at some time. Refusing help could result in property damage, self-injury, and even death in extreme circumstances. If the words are *I will never live in a house like this when I am big*, the vow means if my house becomes "like this" I will get out no matter what. David had a client who demonstrated that "no matter what" meant even if she had to die. She began aging prematurely because of a similarly worded vow. Her hair became brittle and her skin wrinkled, yet she was only in her forties. To the amazement of her doctors, after she completed the homework, her appearance of aging slowed then reversed itself over time. The homework process will be explained in part two.

Words are also important to facilitating a non-judgmental attitude that brings us out of emotional reaction, into understanding, and on to healing. For example, it is far more constructive to view behavior as "working" to create a desired result or "not working" and out of alignment with a desired result. This simple shift enables the practical, adult point of view of what is going on right now as opposed to good or bad (the child thinking) and right or wrong (the parent talking). Sometimes, clients begin to criticize themselves when they realize they created such a "bad" thought. When I remind them that children create beliefs to help themselves survive in the world, but those beliefs don't work well for the adult, they move out of self-condemnation and into healing.

Sometimes children can create vows that are words taken right out of the mouth of a parent to be dutifully obeyed. David, my late husband, was a skinny beanpole when he was a child, as was his older brother Gus. When Gus reached thirty years of age, he started gaining lots of weight, although he hadn't changed his activity level or diet. When David reached thirty, the same thing happened to him. When the brothers talked, they recalled that their mother would often tell them when they were very young, "Just remember, when you get to be thirty, you'll gain lots of weight just like every other man in this family!"

David used the Body Memory Process to free himself of the vow and subsequently lost the extra weight. Although he offered to help his brother through it, Gus did not choose to work on himself and continued to gain weight until his mother died. Within the six months following his mother's passing, Gus lost seventy pounds and kept the weight off for the rest of his life!

In this chapter you will meet Ann, whose vows held her back from fulfilling relationships with her family and friends. You will learn a lot about the nuances that show up in the wording of vows and how even one word in a vow can make a huge difference in someone's behavior and life experiences.

Ann's Story

Ann sat on the couch with a tub of ice cream, staring at the wall. Despite the scream in her head to stop, she couldn't seem to, her hand continuing to move the spoon as if it had a will  of its own. On a quest to lose thirty pounds, she was ten pounds from her goal when she lost her willpower and once again began her old eating patterns. As she contemplated the ten pounds she had quickly regained, Ann wondered why she was able to always snatch defeat from the jaws of victory. Whenever she got close to achieving something she really wanted, something would happen to prevent her from reaching her goal. Either she would sabotage herself, or a looming obstacle would arise and she would give up.

"I hate feeling like such a loser!" Ann thought as she dug in for another bite.

Suddenly, the doorbell rang. Ann jumped up guiltily and shoved the ice cream into the freezer. "I'm coming!" she yelled.

Ann opened the door to her oldest sister, who walked in and gave her a hug without saying anything for a few seconds. "How does she always seem to know when I need a hug?" Ann thought as she sighed and started to cry.

"Oh, honey what is the matter?" Jan asked as she walked immediately over to the couch and patted it for Ann to sit down.

"I screwed it up, Jan. I was doing so great on my diet this time and then I fell off the wagon! It's not just my diet. I screw up everything as soon as it's going well, especially relationships."

Jan sat and listened to her sister for a while before telling her about an amazing session which helped her discover the decisions she made very early in life. "I think this is something that would be good for you to do, Ann. I can give you the number to call. It has really helped me work through the rocky relationship I've always had with Mom."

Ann always found it hard to say "no," which was another thing that irritated her. But this time she felt giving in to her sister's suggestion sounded like a good idea and agreed to book an appointment. When the day came to have her session, Ann came close to canceling, but was determined not to sabotage herself again.

A session always begins with time for the client to discuss what brings them to the Body Memory Process and to talk about what he or she remembers from childhood. As soon as Ann began talking about as far back as she could remember, it was like turning on a faucet.

"There were six of us kids and you would think nobody could feel alone in a family that large, but I did all the time. I was third to come along and the second daughter. My mom fought with my older sister Jan all the time. She told me you and she discovered that Mom used to tell her to "just do it my way" whenever they quarreled. I don't know if Jan did things Mom's way all that much, but *I* certainly did! In fact, my mother and I dress alike and do our hair and makeup the same way. People even say it's hard to tell us apart on the phone!"

"Do you remember wanting to get your mother's attention more when you were little?"

"Oh, yes. Absolutely!"

"Do you think it's possible you observed your mother telling your sister to just do things her way and decided this was how to get your mother's attention?"

Ann looked stunned and said, "Oh, wow! I must have decided to do absolutely everything like her!" We then recorded the vow, *I will be just like you, Mom.*

"Now, Dad was a different story," Ann said with a wry smile. "He was all into my brothers, and I so wanted him to play with me, too. I'd search until I found him, usually in the garage, and ask him lots of questions about what he was doing. He would just tell me to stay out of the way, and a lot of times he'd also say he didn't have time for me and to go play somewhere else. Over time, I guess I realized *I have to stay out of the way* and stopped bothering him."

After acknowledging this as a vow, we talked for a few minutes about "have to" as meaning "don't want to." Let's say I have a big weekend away planned with my family that I'm really looking forward to. On Friday morning my friend calls and says she has two concert tickets for seats near the stage for one of my favorite bands that evening. We have Friday hotel reservations at our weekend getaway location so I tell my friend, "Oh no, I'm sorry but I can't! I have to leave town with my family right after the kids get out of school this afternoon."

Using the words "have to" or "must" implies that now I don't want to go on the weekend trip, because something I'd rather do has come up. This conflict that I create might put me in a bad mood for while or even for the entire weekend. "Have to" robs us of our joy and the realization that we are always at choice.

Ann said, "Oh, gee—I just remembered something else. My mother would tell us older kids we had to love the new baby when there was one expected."

When *I have to love them* was added to Ann's list of vows, we talked about how she has always felt it difficult to decide whom to love and trust. "When you were a child, *I have to love them* meant your younger siblings. As an adult, "them" can refer to anyone with whom you are in a relationship."

Ann revealed that her mother's favorite child was the youngest daughter, and her father clearly didn't want much to do with her. "After everyone has all the attention they want, if there is any energy left, I might get just a little," Ann stated, her voice almost a whisper and higher pitched than usual.

Suddenly, Ann started crying and went on to talk about how she never believed any of her partners truly loved her. I could hear Ann's voice crack a little as she added, "I know when I came along my parents wanted another boy, so I must have been a big disappointment."

After adding to her list of vows, *no one has time for me* and *nobody loves me*, Ann asked me how her strained relationships with her family growing up could have such a strong impact on her relationships as an adult.

"When you are little" I began, "you live in a very small world with a handful of people who are your parents and your siblings. You make decisions about how you are, how they are, and how life is within that small world. When you become an adult and are living in a much, much bigger personal world and out in the big world, those vows still apply. Just like 'them' in *I have to love them, nobody loves me* doesn't just mean you are feeling neglected by your family. *Nobody loves me means* nobody in the big wide world."

Ann was quiet for a few moments, and I was quiet too, letting her sit with the energy that was coming up to meet her intention to discover more explanations for her feelings of failure. Suddenly, Ann jumped up and said, "Wait, if all these vows we are finding have to do with my relationships, what about the fact that I can never seem to reach my goals? That's the main reason I came to meet with you! I was talking with Jan about how I can always seem to steal defeat from the jaws of victory . . . "

"Ann," I said gently. "Yes, we've talked a lot about your relationships with family and friends. What is your relationship with money?"

"Relationship with money? What do you mean? I don't have any relationship with money!" she shrugged. "It comes, it goes . . . hey, just like my boyfriends! Maybe I do have a dysfunctional relationship with money!"

We laughed, and then I explained that money is the resource we first learn about very early in life as we watch how our parents deal with it.

"Oh, I have a very clear memory of Mom telling me all the time that I needed to share my clothes and my toys with my brothers and sisters. She would say to never expect to get what I asked for because the family was large, and we don't have the money to get everybody everything they want."

Once we had identified the vow, *I can't get what I want*, I thought

Ann was going to fall off the couch as she doubled over and laughed so hard. With laughter tears in her eyes, she managed to finally say, "Do you mean to tell me the reason I get close to achieving something then ruin it is because of the vow, *I can't get what I want?* That had to do with a kid asking for a new bicycle, not an adult trying to lose weight!"

"Yes, but as we've discussed, a vow can pertain to one thing for the child but the wording of the vow—if it's allowed to remain in place—will apply to whatever is going on in the adult's life. You could sit down and make a list of what you want and realize *I can't get what I want* has been blocking your efforts to achieve each thing on that list.

After identifying *I can't say no* because child Ann was smacked and told so often, "Don't you tell me NO!" we wrapped up the session. Ann was fascinated by the meaning of various words as they showed up in vows, so I gave her a list:

Always/never . . . adds a degree of absoluteness which allows no latitude or lapse and prohibits any change.

I can't . . . makes one feel powerless when what "I can't" presents itself in life.

I won't . . . takes away choice.

I will . . . takes away choice and creates a default behavior.

I am . . . defines how I perceive and present myself.

I have to . . . creates resentment, yet continuation of the behavior.

He/she/they can't . . . creates resentment and often anger if "they" do what "they can't."

He/she/they are . . . creates expectations (of how he/she/they must be) and, in worse cases, creates blind spots to he/she/they having different opinions, attitudes, and rules about life.

Life is . . . or *This is* . . . creates how the individual interprets life events.

Little . . . added to a vow usually creates the feeling of unimportance or being trivial and without much power.

When I get big/big enough/bigger . . . The concept of "old" or "older" is not understood until after formative childhood years, and this can create weight issues in the adult because they are inadvertently always trying to get "big" to enable or prevent something. Examples are: *When I am big, I will be happy. When I am big enough, he will love me. When I am big, she won't talk to me like that.*

Ann's Vows

VOW	WHEN FORMED/CAUSE	HOW SHOWED UP FOR ANN
I'm not good enough	Birth (parents wanted another son and were disappointed at her birth)	Didn't feel like she deserved any good things in life; whenever something started working, she would wait "for the other shoe to drop"
I have to love them	Child (refers to little brothers and sisters)	Adult Ann was unable to discern who to trust and love
I have to stay out of the way	Child (very often told by her father to stay out of the way)	Adult Ann never asked for anything and seemed to often "hide"
He hurt me	Child (rejection by her father)	Always feared getting hurt in a relationship
I will not be like her	Child (observed her sister, who fought with her mother because she always wanted to do everything her own way)	Ann would go out of her way to ensure she wasn't doing something the way her sister did
I will be just like you, Mom	Child (observed her mother advising her sister to "just do it my way")	Ann and her mother dressed, did makeup and hair alike; even sounded alike on the phone
I can't say no	Child (often smacked and told "Don't you tell me NO!")	Was often taken advantage of and felt out of control because she would not say no and always did what they wanted
I can't get what I want	Child (was told she had to share and "never expect to get" what she wanted)	Could never seem to achieve what she wanted
No one has time for me	Child (constantly rejected when seeking her father's attention)	Says "After everyone has all the attention they want, if there is any energy left, I might get just a little"
Nobody loves me	Child (mother spent all her energy on first-born problem daughter and her favorite youngest daughter; rejected by father)	Ann "ruined" several relationships by not believing her partner loved her—no matter what he did to prove it

Ann's Vow Combinations

1. The combination of *I have to love them, I can't get what I want, nobody loves me,* and *I can't say no* left Ann powerless and seldom fulfilled by her relationships.

2. The opposition between *I will not be like her* and *I will be just like you, Mom* created a very rigid, limited female behavior pattern.

Results in Ann's Life After the Body Memory Process Session and Homework Completion

About six months later, Ann told me she finally believed people when they praised her, and that was a very different experience for her. She said she was in a new relationship and realized she could believe he loved her. Ann stated that after she forgave her mother, she was able to totally re-examine the relationship and decided she did not have to be "just like her" anymore as, "there are a lot of things I do much better than she does."

About a year later she called to tell me the happy news that she had gotten married and was going to have a baby.

Summary of What Ann Learned About the Power of Words in Thought, Belief, and Vow Creation

1. As important as finding the wording of the vow is determining the meaning of that vow in one's life. I could have the vow *they'd rather have someone else* because I perceived the disappointment in my parents at birth (because I was a girl, and they wanted a boy). What the vow means in my life is that I'm constantly suspicious that my boyfriend is cheating on me.

2. Language conveys intention, and by paying attention to our words we can select the ones that can bring us the best chance

of success (such as the difference between "I will try to . . ." and "I will do . . ." something.) Another example is using "have to . . ." which implies we are powerless and not at choice, resulting in negative emotions that can impact our health.

3. Vows are born out of the small world we lived in as children. We were the center of our own world, which was comprised of very few people, mainly our caregivers and family members. Pronouns used in childhood vows originally represent the people in this small world, but for the adult, they represent all people in the entire world of possible relationships.

4. Vows are often about relationships with people, but can also be about often intertwined relationships with abundance, challenges, career, and life. Ann discovered that her difficulties facing any challenge originated with a vow about her relationship with money (abundance).

5. Every word in a vow has meaning and it is important to discover the exact (as possible) wording of the vow. What family member told you that you couldn't do something? Knowing whether it was a male or female member will give you the clue to limitations in your relationships with either men or women.

6. It is far more constructive to view behavior as "working" to create a desired result or "non-working" rather than labeling it as good or bad, or as right or wrong.

Useful Exercises for Integrating What You Learned in This Chapter

1. If you are a parent or teacher or have any opportunity to observe a child, listen for how often he or she uses words like "always" and "never." Young children very often use these words because living in a small world, the infinity of time is a difficult concept to grasp and "always" could actually mean for the past

week. The difficulty arises when the child grows up with the vows that contain these words and now, because words have specific meaning, the vow translates to truly "always" or "never."

2. The next time you take on something new and someone asks what you are doing, say "I'm trying to. . ." then say "I'm _____ ." For example, say, "I'm trying to build a cabinet" and notice how it feels in your body. Notice the person's response. Then in interaction with a different person, say "I'm building a cabinet!" and notice how it feels in your body. Again, notice the person's response.

3. The next time you have an argument with your significant other or need to correct a child, make a statement about what didn't work well instead of telling the person he or she was wrong or bad. Be gentle in your explanation and note how differently the person reacts compared to a time when there were accusations, blame, and guilt involved. Take note of the difference in your own experience of the situation.

CHAPTER FIVE

Mike Realizes the Impact of Birth Trauma on Vow Creation

One of my favorite sitcoms is *Frasier*, and as much as I admire the casting, writing, and performance of the show, one line of an episode left me stunned. Frasier's dad, marveling at the recent birth of a baby remarked, "One minute it's just this blob in some lady's stomach, next minute it's a person!"

I can understand the amazement of seeing the formless blob of a pregnant woman's stomach, then seeing the tiny human form of a newly birthed baby. What I find difficult to understand is the literal notion that a baby isn't a "person" until it is born.

There is no consensus amongst scientists regarding exactly when human life begins. Some say at conception, others say at various points during the gestation period, and still others say not until the baby takes its first breath. Professor of Biology, Scott Gilbert, in his talk on "When Does Personhood Begin?" refers to a statement made by American political philosopher Michael Sandel when he was brought before the President's Commission on Bioethics. Sandel, referring to the extremely high incidence of embryo loss in natural procreation, argues that such loss cannot truly be considered infant death or "pregnancy would have to be regarded as a public health crisis of epidemic proportions."[1]

Sandel could be correct that the ubiquitous failure of a zygote to implant and eventually become a fetus precludes thinking that this is truly a mass loss of human life. If a zygote *does* implant and mature to result in a live birth, however, the bond between mother and baby is strong and present early on. In 2020, Pew biomedical scholars seeking to develop diagnostic and preventative measures to help ensure children live long, healthy lives concluded that the earliest connection between a mother and child is made after a fertilized egg transforms into cells that form the embryo and the placenta.[2]

This earliest connection shows up in what is termed the "conception vow," an energetic conclusion by the baby because of the mother's reaction to learning she is going to have a baby. Think about the moment when a woman finds out she is pregnant. Either she is joyful or fearful, unaware of the impact her intense feelings are already having on the developing life. Let's consider a common conception vow, *I am an accident.* This vow results from the pregnancy being a surprise and can elicit either joy or fear. If the parents had been trying to get pregnant then finally gave up, the vow *I am an accident* can appear to produce positive results. One client reported she could fall into a cesspool and come out "smelling like a rose" because she was so lucky by accident. Most often, those whose conception was "accidental" report being accident-prone, from falls and bumps to more serious issues like a series of car accidents.

That trauma can occur because of the birth process has been a dawning realization since the early 1970s, with the work of Dr. David Chamberlain (*Babies Remember Birth*) and Frederick Leboyer (*Birth Without Violence*). There are now myriad books written on the topic, social media sites, and many support groups available. However, many such resources still only address the trauma experienced by the mother, with no reference to trauma to the baby.

Sometimes a baby can be traumatized by circumstances surrounding the pregnancy, and sometimes those circumstances can even cause a premature birth. In the introduction to this book, I mentioned my distraught birth mother as causing my birth before the end of the second trimester. I don't know a lot about what caused her extreme anxiety, but it probably included someone who constantly raged at her for being pregnant out of wedlock. I believe that when she took a knife to her own abdomen it was more an act of mercy than an attack. In my reality, however, it was an attack, and as a child or even as an adult, sudden bursts of anger aimed at me would make me want to crawl under a table and hide.

Likely related to the confusion over exactly when human life begins, the creators of modern hospital birthing overlooked groundbreaking research, such as that conducted by Dr. David Chamberlain, proving that a newborn baby is aware, can feel pain, and can attempt to communicate its feelings. The low temperature and bright lighting of the delivery room is set to accommodate the medical staff, not the newborn. Drugs are used to accommodate the mother, with no regard for the separation it creates for the baby when Mom suddenly "goes away." The baby is often whisked away by the medical staff for one procedure or another, without regard to the maternal-fetal bond.

More recent birthing practices have been modified in some hospitals to be gentler on the baby. For example, they now rub the baby's back with a warm towel to elicit crying, instead of holding the baby upside down then a slap on the bottom. They no longer administer silver nitrate, now known to be ineffective as well as to cause pain and sometimes great damage to the newborn's eyes. Some delivery rooms are now warmer and dimmer due to an increasing understanding of the impact of birth trauma.

More and more women are refusing drugs at birth because of a realization of the health impact on the child. It is not a coincidence that we began using a lot of drugs in childbirth in the 1940s, then these children who first experienced drugs at birth helped bring about a drug culture that emerged in the late 1950s and early 1960s.

I have heard clients say they were traumatized when they began wondering if they even gave birth because the staff had whisked the baby off somewhere. The result for the baby can be more serious. There is a connection between the baby taken away too soon after birth and addictive behavior later in life. A baby who experiences separation caused by a mother on drugs at birth and being taken away too soon will be especially at risk for drug addiction.

You will next meet Mike, a Body Memory Process client whose birth trauma resulted from his being an unexpected, second-born twin whose mother received drugs at birth.

Mike's Story

Mike stood in front of the café watching his identical twin brother Peter smugly saunter away down the street. In that moment, he wondered why it was always a competition between him and his brother. Peter had just wished him luck in the 5K race they were both entered to run that coming weekend, adding that he could still drop out if he didn't want to be embarrassed by coming in last with the old ladies. Mike wanted to feel angry at Peter for always putting him down, but he wanted more to feel the close connection that he had read most twins feel. Feelings didn't come easily for Mike, and that perplexed him as much as Peter's competitive nature.

It was a little before 7 p.m. when Mike came out of his thoughts and began walking the few blocks to the lot where he was parked. Within a few minutes, he saw an easel sign outside a bookstore advertising a 7 p.m. free introduction to the Body Memory Process. Mike walked up to the sign to read the attached flyer, "Come learn how birth trauma and early life decisions can be causing difficulties in your life."

He didn't have anything else planned for the evening, so he went in and sat in the back. As he listened, Mike became increasingly convinced that he needed to book a session to explore why he always found it so hard to stand up to Peter and assert himself in other areas of his life.

That Saturday afternoon, Mike began by explaining to me how neglected he thought he was while growing up. He admitted that being in such a large family of ten made individual attention difficult, but said he always thought everyone else got just a little more than he did.

"It wasn't so much that I felt sad because I was neglected. I've never been able to feel as much as others seem to. It was more of an observation and a thought that I didn't get as much as everyone else."

This statement raised a red flag for me, and I asked Mike if he knew any specifics about his birth, including whether his mother had received drugs. He said he didn't, and I asked him to talk with his mom after the session and to give me a call to discuss what he learned. A few days later I received a call from Mike, who began with, "You're not going to believe this!"

Mike said his mother was surprised by his question, but he explained that he was working on himself, and that it was important to learn about his birth. Mike said his mother explained that she was given a drug and told she shouldn't feel anything. Her body reaction, however, was not typical and she felt everything. She said she couldn't think straight or tell the medical staff what was going on. She just kept thinking "I shouldn't feel anything." Mike was amazed when I explained that his vow, *I shouldn't feel anything*, was the reason he found it difficult to normally experience feelings and be sympathetic to others.

During the session, after Mike mentioned his thought of being neglected, he went on to explain how he focused his desire for more attention on his identical twin brother, Peter. "I fixated on being better than Peter because I was convinced that was the way to get more attention. But Peter always seemed to get what he wanted. Peter was always faster and stronger than me, so if there wasn't a lot of something, he would beat me to it and take it all for himself. It wasn't until we were grown that Peter admitted to me that one Christmas when we were ten, he had learned about an afternoon party a neighbor was having and that they were giving presents to the neighborhood kids. Peter said he kept the party a secret from me, went to get his gift, and then came back to impersonate me so that he could get my gift, too."

After hearing more about Mike's birth, including his parents not knowing they had twins until the birth and Mike being born second, we discovered the vows *I will do anything I have to so you'll see me* and *I have to beat him.* When I explained that "have to" usually means "don't want to," Mike shouted, "Yes! I can remember thinking when I was a kid that it shouldn't bug me that Peter got so much, and I got so little. I was resentful that I felt so compelled to compete with him."

When I asked Mike if anything else was compelling him to work on himself, he replied immediately, "Yes. I am tired of being so unobtrusive and quiet. If I go somewhere and have a good time, afterwards I'm always beating myself up for talking too much. If I'm the center of attention, even for a short period of time, I berate myself for that, too."

As a child, Mike was often told "don't bother me," then pushed away. He was also told he was too loud. After talking about this for a while, we added the vows *I won't bother anybody* and *I am too loud* to the list.

"How about this?" Mike suddenly asked. "I will never talk about my feelings. I know I haven't really had a lot of them—even if I hurt myself! Someone can ask if I need help and I can be bleeding all over the place and still say I'm OK!"

"Do you know if your mother had any scares when she was pregnant with you?"

"I remember her telling me that she was in a car accident when she was close to delivering me. She wasn't too badly hurt—just bruised legs and some back pain for a while. She did say she was really scared about me."

"She likely was praying that you be OK—or asking you to be OK, which is why you have a vow that typically reflects as *I'm fine* or *I'm OK.* We see this mostly with firstborns when the mother experiences a jolt or a fall and is especially vigilant and worried because it is her first pregnancy. But it can also happen with any pregnancy if the scare is bad enough. Dr. Kevin Leman talks about this in *The New Birth Order Book* when he discusses firstborn characteristics."

We wrapped up the session with a reminder to Mike to call me after he'd talked with his mom. Afterwards, we completed his list of vows with *I shouldn't feel anything*.

Mike's Vows

VOW	WHEN FORMED/CAUSE	HOW SHOWED UP FOR MIKE
I will be a boy	Womb (parents wanted a boy)	He was a boy; no issues reported
I will do anything I have to so you'll see me *I have to beat him*	Infant/Child (always thought he had to be better than his brother to get even a little attention)	Always felt he had to get someone at something to get what should be "rightfully his"
I won't bother anybody	Child (told "don't bother me" and pushed away)	Very unobtrusive and said he needed lessons on asserting himself
I am too loud	Child (often told he was too loud and quiet was to be accepted)	Was very quiet and constantly berating himself for talking too much or being center of attention
When I am bigger someone will love me	Child (felt he never got enough attention as a child; felt everyone got just a little more than he did)	Whenever he felt unloved he gained weight
I am the wrong one	Birth (they were not expecting him so his brother got the name they had planned for a boy)	Always felt out of place and spent a lot of time wondering what was going to happen to him "when the right person shows up"
I shouldn't feel anything	Birth (mother's thought during birthing, as doctor told her this after giving her birth drugs)	Stated he was very insensitive—not only to others; he wouldn't feel the emotions other people felt
I am OK	Womb (mother in accident in third trimester and scared for the baby)	Won't talk about the feelings he does have

Mike's Vow Combinations

1. Combine *I am too loud* and *I won't bother anybody* and the cause of Mike's lack of self-assertion is obvious.

2. Combine *I will do anything I have to so you'll see me* and *I won't bother anybody* create strong opposition. The *I won't bother anybody* became predominant because it was reinforced by *I am too loud*.

Results in Mike's Life After the Body Memory Process Session and Homework Completion

I saw Mike about six months later, and he introduced his twin. Peter, obviously used to being the dominant twin, told me that Mike had taken an assertiveness training. Mike gently corrected Peter, saying "Tell her about *your* life."

The pregnant pause demonstrated how shocking Peter found this unusual behavior. Mike continued, "After I let go of all that baggage, I needed tools. I found I can be assertive *and* gentle."

He looked at Peter and said to me, "And—it really gets attention!" He then turned to me and said, "I get to be me, not a carbon copy." Mike patted his brother on the back saying, "Everything—my job, my relationships, even being his twin just plain feels better!"

Summary of What Mike Learned About Womb and Birth Trauma

1. Trauma can occur as early as when the mother finds out she is pregnant. This is considered "conception trauma" because this is when the connection has already been established between the new life and the mother—after the fertilized egg transforms into cells that form the embryo and the placenta. Trauma can occur when the mother is fearful about being pregnant and can even have thoughts about having an abortion. Some typical

conception vows are *I am an accident* (unplanned), *it's all my fault* (I caused this fear), and *sex is bad* (because that happened and now this happened, and nobody is happy about it).

2. Womb trauma is facilitated by the deep connection between the developing baby and the mother. The baby will energetically perceive any expectations by the parents as well as "family jewels," or vows passed from one generation to the next. Examples are *I will be a boy for you* (often Dad's expectation of a boy), *I am fine* (caused by an incident that makes Mom afraid for the baby), and *I have to take care of everything myself* (if Mom is feeling unsupported).

3. Traditional birthing practices have created many opportunities for birth trauma due to the surprise and discomfort felt by the baby being born, after spending so much time in a warm, comfortable space connected to the mother. Examples are *something must be wrong with me* (gender surprise at birth or a need for sudden, life-saving techniques), *if I don't get out of here, I am going to die* (baby feeling stuck in the birth canal), and *he/she hurts me* (depending on whether the offending doctor is male or female).

4. Often, the most deeply held vows are created during the birth process. The strongest and most pattern-creating vows I encounter are those of the birth script. There are countless examples of people struggling for the first thirty or forty years of life, even their entire life, with the misinformation they received during birth. In the rebirthing community, this is often referred to as the "birth lie" and is the biggest lie we believe about ourselves. Birth vows can be accepted instantly from one statement in the delivery room (such as *there's nothing special about this one*, meaning simply "this is a textbook case"), and from this, the individual constructs a behavior pattern—often for life. Birth thoughts are also often seen in how we handle stress.

5. The use of drugs at birth can create a lot of problems when the baby suddenly feels disconnected from the mother or the mother is present and confused (such as the drug not working as it should and Mike's mother repeating in her mind, *I shouldn't feel anything*).

Useful Exercises for Integrating What You Learned in This Chapter

1. Floating Exercise

   Let's use our imaginations to consider the contrast between the environment of the baby in utero and in a delivery room. As you sit there, please close your eyes and imagine your body floating suspended in space. Create the space so that you have no sense of gravity pulling at you. Eliminate all the usual touch sensations of your body, such as the backs of your legs touching the chair. Imagine that there are only the very faintest of sounds that occasionally penetrate your space. Imagine only the very weakest light in this space. What remains is you and your thoughts. At first, your logical mind just notices the loss of stimulation, that there is no information from the outside. Just continue to float suspended in space. As you notice and complete each thought, suddenly you notice the quiet; not just the quiet of no stimulation but the profound quiet of a still mind.

   Now we are going to extend this process for an hour or, better yet, two. The way we do this is called a sensory deprivation or float tank. So, climb into the float tank and notice what happens. You lie in water on your back, your body floating suspended in space with no sense of gravity. The water and air are the perfect temperature, so you stop noticing hot or cold and touch. There is little or no sound or light. What is left is you and your thoughts. At first, your logical mind just notices the loss of stimulation; that there is no information from the outside. Thoughts of fear may surface, and you might wonder if you have been forgotten. You may feel trapped and want to check the door, and you may open your eyes. Then, as you settle down and experience each thought, you notice a clearing of involvement with day-to-day concerns. You notice the quiet of no stimulation and move into the profound quiet of a still mind. After two hours in the float tank, most people have an experience of deep clarity of purpose and direction, and it is possible to see the solutions to many of life's complex problems in the quiet of one's own mind. This is the environment of the baby in utero.

What happens if we again extend the time of this process to months? All we know for months and months is the encompassing feeling of love. It is after months of being in this space that you can encounter the harsh environment of a brightly lit, noisy, much colder delivery room.

2. If you already know the circumstances of your birth, take some time to write that down. Since you will have the opportunity later in this book to discover your own childhood vows, which will include gathering all known information on your time in the womb and your birth, this is a good opportunity to get a head start—during this time of learning about womb and birth vows. If you don't know the circumstances of your birth, talk with your mother if she is available, or other family members who might have been present.

3. Do the same process for your time in the womb. What have you been told? What can you learn from your parents and other family members? Write down all you can pull together.

PART II

HOW TO STOP BELIEVING IT

CHAPTER SIX

Discovering Your Pain Points

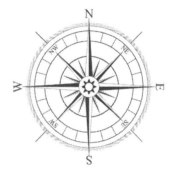

If you were out for a drive and wanted to redirect your course, what would be important to know? First, the motivation to make a change comes from a realization that the road you are on isn't taking you where you want to go. Next, you would need to determine the road that *will* take you where you want to go. You would also want to know which road you are on so that you could navigate to the new route.

How do you know if you need to make a personal course correction? Look at the results in your life. Are you well, successful, happy, and prosperous? Are you achieving your goals and realizing your dreams? If not, then the road you are on isn't taking you where you want to go. It's not the traffic, other travelers who are getting in your way and slowing you down. It's not the type of road or the way it winds that slows you down, either. It is as if you are trapped on a highway with no visible exits.

In part one, you learned that children form core beliefs while they are determining what is necessary to survive in the world. They are, essentially, creating a map for navigating life. However, because they make very emotional conclusions about themselves and others based on extremely limited information, they draw one piece at a time. Children are fixated on how to survive, not *thrive*, so the information is tactical and not all connected into a comprehensive, strategic plan for life. We can feel stuck in a single, confusing behavior pattern with no visible way out. The good news is that you can become aware of the road you are currently on, reaffirm where you want to go, and use an unfailing system of navigation to recalculate and correct your course!

In part two, you will learn how to discover your own childhood vows, and then how to do the homework to release them. The self-discovery process will involve a 360-degree look at your life to see where you might have hidden vows to reveal and release. This chapter will prime you for that work as you continue to read about the journeys of clients who uncovered vows relating to specific areas of their lives.

All the clients who came to the Body Memory Process had noticed several things that were not working in their lives. They came to the work already having taken a huge step, which is to avoid the temptation to blame others for their problems. The idea that their problems were connected to early life experiences and beliefs resonated deeply with them. They came to their session with a strong intention to find the root cause and a commitment to do the work necessary to free themselves of what was not serving them.

You will see from all the case studies in this book that this must be a self-discovery process, because you are a unique individual with an inimitable set of circumstances while in the womb, at birth, and in your early childhood. Finding your childhood vows will likely be an iterative process as you make one discovery to then reach back further to find more information and clues to other vows. The first step will be looking for all the pain points in your life now, across the spectrum of your relationships with yourself, with others, and with your resources.

Sometimes the message that change is needed is loud and clear, and sometimes it shows up subtly, in non-working relationships. The way that vows show up in people's lives is as diverse as people themselves. One common thread is that everything is about relationships—how you think, feel, and either irrationally react or consciously act in relationship to everything in your life. You have a relationship with your body, your mind, your spirit, your voice, others, money, time, and choice.

You are at the center of each of these connections, and each of them can be greatly impacted by the vows you made early in life—formed around the people you were first in relationships with. The good news is that you can change yourself and make a huge positive impact on every single relationship.

Resources, such as money and time, are external, but your relationship to them is very much a personal, internal experience. You might think you can't control the flow of money to you, but you are absolutely in control of your attitudes and practices around your finances. Whether you think money coming in is a trickle or a waterfall is up to you. How you spend or save it is up to you.

You can perceive time as moving too quickly or too slowly, and this can vary depending on what you are doing. Maybe you never think you have enough time to get the things done that you want to do. You might find yourself always early or always late, and if you absolutely must be on time, you might get upset if you are late. Perhaps you are a procrastinator and consistently put things off, which makes you always feel behind. Your attitudes about money came from observing your parents' attitudes about money. Your relationship with time is largely about your birth script and whether you were born early, late, or on time.

In addition to what you learned from the clients discussed in part one, the following brief case studies will demonstrate how more clients have discovered the vows that were impacting the various relationships in their lives. Please note, to avoid repetition, "typical vows" such as *I'm fine* and *he hurt me* will not be included in these case studies—unless they had special significance to the client.

Client Jack

Jack's main relationship issues were with his wife, his boss, his voice (self-expression), and time (issues under time pressure).

His vows included:

1. *If I don't get out of here, I'm going to die*, caused by his very held back then long birth. Because of this vow, Jack tended to panic under pressure.

2. *I am separate*, caused by his mother's severe post-partum and relatively long use of birth drugs. Infant Jack was emotionally neglected and was able to confirm that because of a bad reaction to the birth drugs, he wasn't reunited with his mother until four days after his birth. Jack felt disconnected from his wife and often had the irrational fear he was going to lose her.

3. *What is wrong with me* was caused by the birth trauma of being held back—which wasn't because of anything wrong with the baby, but because the doctor was running late. Jack always thought there was something wrong with him.

4. *I can't do anything*, caused by his father telling him this when he was little because he had no patience with him. Adult Jack always needed personal guidance at work.

5. *I can't tell the truth*, caused by his father telling him "you can't tell the truth" whenever his impression didn't match what child Jack was saying. Jack couldn't talk about his feelings and always believed something bad would happen if he told the truth about what was going on for him.

6. *I'll do it my way* was in place because Jack rebelled against his father by deciding he would do things his way. Jack said he got into a lot of trouble with his superiors because they perceived that he couldn't take direction.

Jack's vows, *I can't do anything* and *I'll do it my way* were in opposition. Seeking mentorship and guidance illuminated for Jack's bosses the fact that he wasn't following the guidance because he wanted to do things his way.

After completing the homework, Jack said he finally felt good about himself. He received a promotion at work once his supervisor was convinced that he believed he could do the new job. Jack said he felt a lot closer to his wife and no longer worried about losing her. During his discovery work, he found out his mother had experienced a very bad reaction to the birth drugs and that he was not able to reconnect with her until the fourth day after his birth.

Client Tom

Tom's main relationship issues were with women, his brother, and his self-expression, as well as all relationships that might include confrontation with or direction from others.

His vows included:

1. *I'm the wrong one,* which was caused by a family joke since his birth, because Tom looked very different than his parents, that they had gotten the babies mixed up at the hospital. Tom always questioned his appropriateness, and fitting in was always a problem in any situation. He was always "looking for the right one to come take my place." It was so difficult for him to believe that he was loved that he ruined two marriages with jealousy, having always demanded that they love him "his way."

2. *I can't know that* was caused by being told he couldn't possibly know what he intuitively knew from an early age. This vow was so strong in his life that Tom wasn't interested in anything that wasn't provable. He didn't like fiction or movies and had a difficult time expressing himself.

3. *She can't yell at me* came from Tom's mother yelling at him when she was upset, which would get his father upset if it woke him up, resulting in his receiving corporal punishment from his father. He couldn't stand being yelled at and would do everything he could to avoid upsetting females.

4. *I'll hide* was a method of coping with upsetting his mother and adult Tom hid from any confrontation in relationships.

5. *I should be seen and not heard* came from early childhood turmoil and caused problems with Tom's self-expression.

6. *You can't make me do what you want* came from Tom always being told to not let others tell him what to do. His most vivid early childhood memory was being "led into trouble by an older girl," and he always tended to question females and their motives.

7. *I have to be perfect* was a coping mechanism for dealing with emotional parents and Tom admitted to being a "failed perfectionist."

8. *I have to tell the truth* was a constant message for the entire family and what is considered to be a "family jewel." Tom was always brutally honest when asked a direct question, and said he even scared himself because he would be so abrupt in blurting out the point.

Tom's vow combinations are a great demonstration of how vows can individually cause issues, and combined cause havoc:

1. Combine *I'll hide, I'm the wrong one*, and *I should be seen and not heard*, and the roots of Tom's feelings of powerlessness and lack of fulfillment in relationships are clear.

2. Combine *I have to be perfect* with *I will be still, I will be quiet, I should be seen and not heard, I am the wrong one*, and *I can't know that* and Tom's "yes man" label is further complicated with "analysis paralysis" and procrastination.

3. Combine *you can't make me do what you want* with all Tom's
    other vows about relationships and understand how he would
    try to be totally passive.

4. Combine *I have to tell the truth* with Tom's relationship and
    work-related vows and the result is Tom hides and avoids and
    is still unless asked a direct question. Then he is brutally honest
    and this all contributes to his breakdown in social graces.

After completing the homework, Tom reported that he had made
several changes. He had told a "social lie," was enrolled in Dale Car-
negie to learn public speaking, and had decided to find a better job.
He had several very good talks with his girlfriend, and everything
was better in his relationship. He had stopped obsessing over his
second wife and his relationships with all three of his children were
greatly improved.

Client Julia

Julia's main relationship issues were with men and self-expression.
Her vows include:

1. *I will always be your good little girl, Mom* came from early
    childhood.

2. *I will be a boy* was a womb vow and Julia reported being a
    tomboy.

3. *When I'm big enough she won't yell* was a decision Julia made
    as a child because her mother yelled a lot. Julia had a lot of
    weight problems and increased eating when she was yelled at.

4. *I don't trust men* came from Julia's mother not trusting her
    father, and Julia had no relationships at all for several years.

5. *It's all my fault* is a typical vow due to life changes for the mother.
    Julia tended to blame herself for everything.

6. *She hates me* came from Julia's mother being angry about

changes in her life due to pregnancy. Julia could not relate to her mother or any older female.

7. *Sex is bad* came from being an accident, and Julia could only enjoy sex as one-night stands.

8. *I'll be quiet* came from the house always being very loud, so Julia found she could get attention by being quiet, after which her mother would ask "What's wrong?"

9. *He's not around much* was due to Julia's father not being around much. Julia didn't expect any man in her life to stay around long.

10. *Men are not very important* came from her mother constantly trying to separate her from her father because she was jealous of their relationship. Julia had no relationships for a long time.

11. *When I'm old enough I'll find love* is what Julia was told by her father. Julia never seemed to be old enough, though, and spent a long time waiting to be old enough for a relationship.

12. *I don't matter* was due to her mother having a very low opinion of females. Julia always believed she didn't matter.

Julia had two vows in opposition: *I will always be your good little girl, Mom* and *I will be a boy*. She had extreme problems with puberty and problems with male/female patterning, because she was a "girl" not a woman. Whenever the "little girl" vow was called forth, she said the boy vow would "go crazy" and vice versa.

Julia reported putting much more effort into making herself attractive after doing the homework and she was even starting to date. She was also no longer avoiding responsibility, which she had previously associated with guilt and blame.

Client Gloria

Gloria's relationship issues were primarily with her mother and with her body.

1. *I'll be OK* came from Gloria's mother falling down the steps during her third trimester and breaking her tailbone.

2. *Whatever you do, I'll be OK* was in place because Gloria's mother was in a lot of pain and on painkillers. She was also worried a lot about the baby. Gloria expected very little attention and support from her spouse and friends, and was so independent she couldn't keep a friend for long.

3. *I will never cause any trouble* was due to the painful pregnancy and her mother's thought that "this one (pregnancy) is a lot of trouble." Gloria went to extremes to avoid confrontation.

4. *You can't yell at me* is because Gloria's mother was a "yeller" whenever she was angry. Child Gloria did everything to please her mother so that she wouldn't yell at her. Adult Gloria had extreme pain in her shoulders whenever someone yelled at her.

5. *I will be funny* was in place because it was Gloria's father's way of diffusing a tense situation when her mother was angry. Gloria would use humor to keep people from getting angry and often would not express what was really going on for her.

6. *I will be strong* came from Gloria's mother being hurt when pregnant with her and being strong was Gloria's way of going through life.

7. *I'll be what you want me to be* was due to the way Gloria used to get attention as the fifth child. Gloria described herself as a "situational chameleon," and her biggest fear was a party where they invited friends and co-workers. She knew she was very different around different groups and feared everyone would find out "the truth."

8. *I will always be happy* was the way Gloria thought she needed to be in order to keep her mother from being angry at her. It was related to her father making jokes, and adult Gloria expressed a lot of false happiness to cover up her true feelings.

9. *I am a cripple* came from her mother's accident during the third trimester. Gloria had no physical handicaps of any kind, yet always thought of herself as being deficient compared to everyone else—a cripple.

Gloria had vow combinations and vows in opposition:

1. Combine *I will be strong* and *I will never cause any trouble* with *nobody will take care of me* and it explains why Gloria thought that anyone who must be taken care of is a weak person; since she had to take care of herself, she thought she was weak.

2. Combine *I will be funny, I will never cause any trouble,* and *I will be what you want* and it is clear why Gloria had a powerful need to make people happy and to please others.

3. Oppose *I will never cause any trouble* and *I will be strong* with *I am a cripple* and it explains Gloria's self-loathing.

Gloria reported that after she finished the homework, she had a dream that made her realize for the first time in her life she didn't think her body was going to fail her. She learned to love her body, stop her panic attacks when she felt pressure, mended her relationship with her mother, moved to a city she always wanted to live in, and eventually became an apprentice of the Body Memory Process.

Client Barry

Barry's relationship issues were primarily with his parents, his wife, and his son.

1. *I will not be alone* was about Barry's family moving to the U.S. fifteen days before his birth. His mother would not let any family member out of her sight during labor and she would not let Barry be taken out of her sight, even for the traditional post-birth bath.

2. *I will mind my own business* was a family jewel. Barry's mother

felt very isolated by the cultural differences and told him people would not like him because he was "too curious and nosy." Barry's father told him many times that "people should mind their own business and that is the way to get along." Barry had great difficulty with intimacy.

3. *I will make them happy* was due to Barry being told repeatedly that he should make his mother and father happy. Barry stated that he never did what pleased himself unless it pleased someone else, too.

4. *I will take care of them* came from Barry being constantly told to take care of his younger brothers and sisters. Adult Barry was the family caretaker. Whenever someone had a problem, he was the one they looked to for a solution. His wife constantly told him he had to create some space with his birth family and complained that "if they stub their toes, you are right there to carry them home."

Barry's vow combinations were:

I will take care of them, I will make them happy, and *I will mind my own business,* which caused a very high stress level when he was around his family.

Add to that mix *I will not be alone* and the need to have them around becomes the reason for exposing himself to all the stress.

The further combination that includes *I have to do it myself* creates the unwillingness of "have to" and a high level of self-blame if "they" are not happy or taken care of.

Months later, I was introduced to Barry's wife and his teenage son. He asked if his son was too young to do a session, and both his wife and son wanted to experience this life-altering work after witnessing the changes in Barry.

Barry said, "You are not going to believe this, but I have really disconnected from my birth family."

He spent some time talking about the chaos in his birth family, how detrimental it was to him and his wife and son, and how compelled he had felt to "fix" all his birth family members. Barry had begun telling his birth family "no" to bailing them out of every problem.

Useful Exercises for Integrating What You Learned in This Chapter

1. Take an honest 360-degree look at your life to determine if you want to make a course correction. Are you well, successful, happy, and prosperous? Are you achieving your goals and realizing your dreams? When you identify what you'd like to change, resist the temptation to identify the cause in the external world. For example, if you are not truly happy at your job, don't blame your boss or even the job you are in. Once you do your discovery work, you might realize you don't need to change anything but yourself. Once you've changed yourself, then you can reassess the need for any external changes.

2. If you didn't already do this while reading through the case studies in this chapter, revisit any that resonated with your own life and any similar issues you've noticed. Start thinking about your own relationship with your parents, siblings, and others who were present in your early life. If you start jotting things down now, you'll have a great head start on your self-discovery process later on!

3. Make a list of all the important relationships in your life that you can think of. Include your relationship with yourself and every person, place, and thing that has significance to your thoughts, feelings, and emotions. Save this list for more self-discovery work later on.

CHAPTER SEVEN

The Body Map

Do you remember the days before ubiquitous GPS access? Folded paper maps or map books were our only, sometimes frustrating, tools. Then there were the places we'd visit without any maps, and the casting back and forth that would occur. I guess a paper map is better than no map, but the best tool is a navigation system that knows where you are at all times and is continually updated with new information.

That is your body—the best, most reliable system for navigating life's challenges. It is important to take some time to honestly assess whether you treat your body as your best friend or as your worst enemy. Unfortunately, most people fight and disparage their body. We struggle with weight issues, wrinkles, and aches and pains. Instead of listening to its helpful messages and living a healthy lifestyle, we tune it out and seek relief through diets, surgery, and medications. As mentioned earlier, Dr. Candace Pert discovered the dramatic interaction of the body with the mind at the molecular level and believed deeply that our body is our subconscious mind. If we want to know what is in the submerged part of the iceberg, all we need to do is look at, listen to, and feel what is going on inside.

In this chapter, you will learn all about the basics of the Body Memory Process Body Map© that was created by David William Sohn after years of working with clients. This map has become a powerful tool for helping people identify their childhood vows through clues provided by their body. You will be using these map basics later on to help you decode your own body's messages. You will also see information on the back cover on how you can access the full version of the Body Memory Process Body Map$^{©}$ which consists of hundreds of vows and where they usually show up in the body.

Over the years of working with clients, David noticed patterns emerge—a correlation between his clients' vows and their consistent reflection as pain and tension in certain areas of the body. If a vow was about communication it would show up as tension, pain, and even disease in the region of the throat or neck—not just for one person, but for every person with a communication vow. Other vows could appear at multiple areas depending upon the impact of that vow on the client's life. For example, finances are very much about security, and thus vows related to finances could be reflected in the root chakra area of the body. But issues around finances could also have a big impact on personal power, and thus could also reflect in the power chakra area of the body.

Massage therapists might notice this too, as when they are massaging a certain sore area, they are activating the body memory and the client might start talking about the same issue/s every time that area is massaged. David found a correlation between the chakras, or energy centers of the body, as well as how vows showed up on the front, the back, or the sides of the body.

I'll tell a story about one of my own experiences of the powerful body map, and then we will dive into each aspect of the tool. For as long as I could recall, I had a large painful knot in my left scapula, or shoulder blade area of my back. If I went to a Western medical doctor with this symptom, I would likely be told it was because I worked at a desk job and perhaps didn't have the best posture when sitting for long periods of time looking at a computer. Maybe I needed to adjust the height of my chair. I might be given a pain cream or pills, and just possibly be referred to a massage therapist. I did try massage, which would provide some relief, but before long the pain would return.

Using the Body Memory Process Body Map,$^{©}$ I was able to quickly decode what was going on, and after I finished my Body Memory

Process homework, I no longer experienced the knot. Here is what I learned by using the map:

- The pain that was in my back and the back side of the body is about how the world relates to me.

- The pain was on the left side of my body, which is about a powerful female in my life.

- The pain was between my communication and heart chakras.

- The pain was about how a powerful woman in my life communicated love to me.

Sure enough, I had a mother who loved me deeply and her expression of love often showed up as being demanding, controlling, and offering only conditional love. If I tried to assert myself, I was often manipulated into feeling guilty until I changed my plans. In my mother's reality, she really wanted me to be safe and thought the only way she could protect me was to coerce me to do things her way. She also really liked my company and didn't want me to spend holidays with anyone but her and my father (before I was married). I remember telling her one year that I wanted to spend Thanksgiving with a friend instead of going home that year. In return, I received a lot of crying and disappointment from my mother with statements like, "What do you expect your father and me to do if you don't come home for Thanksgiving?"

I was also told that if I didn't come home, she would not speak to me again until she wasn't upset any longer.

Once I understood the pain in my back, not only was I able to heal it, I had a new level of understanding of my mother and was able to separate her emotional baggage from my own experiences. From then on, I could take ownership of what was my reality and what was my mom's. I was finally able to release the unhealthy emotional enmeshment between us.

The Body Memory Process Body Map© (referred to from here on as "body map tool") integrates the understanding of how the body presents energy blockages at the level of each of the chakras, or energetic channels of the body, and in the front or back of the body, and on the right or left side of the body.

The Body Axes Involved in the Body Map

Sagittal Plane—The sagittal plane divides the body into left and right halves. The right half is where vows about a powerful male in your life show up. The left half is where vows about a powerful female in your life show up. You might have seen a reference before to the right side of the body being the masculine side, which is about logic, being analytical, being structured, systems approaches, initiating, and doing. The left side of the body is the feminine side, which is about emotions, relationships, intuition, the abstract, feeling, and receiving.

Frontal Plane—The frontal plane divides the body into front and back halves. The front half is where vows about how I relate to the world show up. The back half is where you will find vows about how the world relates to me.

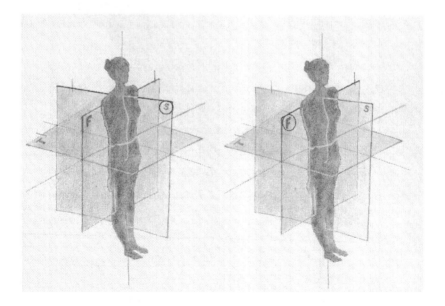

The Chakra System of the Human Body

There is much information available on the internet about the chakra system, which you can consult if you wish to learn more than these basics. Different sources may take slightly different perspectives, but there is consensus on the fundamental aspects of each of the seven major chakras of the body, which is provided here as most pertinent to the body map tool.

The term 'chakra' comes from Sanskrit, the root language of all languages of India, and knowledge of the body's energy centers dates back to ancient Hindu teachings. In Sanskrit, chakra means "wheel" or "disk." A clear and balanced chakra vibrating with a free flow of energy is desirable, and each chakra interacts with each of the others as a system. The cells of the body, themselves always vibrating and reflecting our state of well-being, are impacted by the state of the chakras.

According to chakra expert Dr. Deepak Chopra, "Chakras store the energy of thoughts, feelings, memories, experiences, and actions. They influence and direct our present and future mindset, behavior, emotional health, and actions."

As you learn about each of the seven major chakras of the body, you will see information for each on the Sanskrit name, meaning, color, symbol, location, function, manifestation of unbalanced state, and vow manifestation. You will also see areas of the body regulated by each chakra and examples of vows that could cause energy blockages and tension, pain, or disease in these areas.

Please note that the information associated with chakras and their associated glands and organs is information that has been available for thousands of years, originating in ancient India. In recent history there have been numerous books on the subject.

First, Root Chakra

The Sanskrit name of the first chakra is Muladhara, meaning "base." It is red and symbolized by a lotus flower with four petals. The first chakra regulates the feet, knees, hips, nails, teeth, rectum, and lower spine. It is located at the base of the spine/pubic bone area and its function is  connection to the earth in a body. It also deals with the fundamental survival needs of food, water, shelter, health, and safety. In an unbalanced state we might feel ungrounded and unstable, and we may neglect our physical needs.

Three examples of disease manifestation at this chakra are:

1. Knee problems from vows about making someone proud of them, such as *I have to make them proud of me.*

2. Hip issues from vows causing feelings of shame and guilt which is the cause of all imbalances; hip degeneration is caused by deep-seated shame.

3. Chronic coccyx/tailbone pain caused by someone's physical or emotional sense of survival being challenged.

This chakra is heavily involved in vow formation as the child grows and learns about the world and forms their core beliefs about survival. Vows connected to the root chakra are foundational to the way one lives their life, safety, and what one must do to obtain love and attention.

Some examples of vows associated with the first chakra:

First Chakra/Front of Body	First Chakra/Back of Body
What's the point in trying	*They are not ready for me*
Life is hard	*They did not plan me*
Life is not fair	*Life is a struggle*

Second, Sacral Chakra

The Sanskrit name of the second chakra is Svadhishthana, meaning "dwelling place of the self." It is orange and symbolized by a lotus flower with six petals. The second chakra regulates the reproductive system, kidneys, adrenal system, bladder large intestine, and low back. It is located in

SVADHISHTHANA

the lower abdomen and its function is creativity in all forms, including the creative act of bringing in a new human life. In an unbalanced state, we might be blocked in our ability to be creative and to see the beauty in the creation of others. Vows connected to the sacral chakra are about all aspects of creativity, including sex and relationships.

Three examples of disease manifestation at this chakra are:

1. Bladder problems, from holding on to vows about not letting go or not forgetting or forgiving.

2. Adrenal problems related to defeatism and vows about not being able to care for the self, usually causing pain or injury in a repeated specific location, which keeps the adrenal gland working overtime, often leading to adrenal problems.

3. Sacral/low back pain involves vows about having to do everything myself such as *If I want it done right I have to do it myself.*

Some examples of vows associated with the second chakra:

Second Chakra/Front of Body	Second Chakra/Back of Body
I will always make it better	*When I'm big enough I'll do what I want*
He only wants me for sex	*It is better to be a boy*
I made a mess	*Touch is bad*

Third, Solar Plexus Chakra

The Sanskrit name of the third chakra is
Manipura, meaning "lustrous gem." It is
yellow and symbolized by a lotus flower
with ten petals. The third chakra regulates
the abdomen, small intestines, spleen, liver,
pancreas, stomach, and gallbladder. It is
located at the solar plexus area and its

MANIPURA

function is personal power, self-esteem, and knowing our place in
the world. In an unbalanced state, we might be too concerned about
the opinions of others, be overly sensitive, and lack confidence. Vows
connected to the solar plexus chakra are related to relationships with
others in regarding one's sense of personal power.

Three examples of disease manifestation at this chakra are:

1. Stomach issues are associated with the inability to "stomach"
    something or assimilate something new, with vows associated
    with personal power.

2. Liver problems due to chronic complaining and feeling bad;
    vows specifically affecting liver function are most often self-
    directed. Examples are *I always lose* or *I never get anything my
    way.*

3. Gallbladder disease due to unresolved anger with vows such
    as *I have to get angry to get my way* or *I will try not to be angry.*

Some examples of vows associated with the third chakra:

Third Chakra/Front of Body	Third Chakra/Back of Body
There is never quite enough for me	*He thinks I'm worthless*
I am helpless	*He hurts me and she says it's OK*
There is nothing special about me	*When she's mad I'm wrong*

Fourth, Heart Chakra

The Sanskrit name of the fourth chakra is Anahata, meaning "unhurt" or "unbeaten." It is green and symbolized by a lotus flower with twelve petals. The fourth chakra regulates the hands, shoulders, breasts, upper back, lungs, heart, and thymus. It is located in the middle of the chest at the level  of the heart and its function is unconditional love. In an unbalanced state, we might be unable to have compassion for others and be disconnected from our feelings regarding ourselves, others, and life. Vows connected to the heart chakra are about love and the expression of love to and from others.

Three examples of disease manifestation at this chakra are:

1. Heart attack from squeezing all the joy out of the heart in favor of something else; from vows about something being more important than love, such as *nothing matters but money.*

2. Lung problems due to depression, fear of taking in life, and feelings of unworthiness; most breathing problems relate to vows about the lack of desire to live if certain circumstances occur.

3. Breast problems from vows about "being last" or giving something up to be a mother; also, many breast problems result from keeping secrets, as per the pattern of the pectorals, originating at the throat chakra and ending under the arm. (Note: My mother died from breast cancer that metastasized to her skeletal system. She had struggled for years with how to tell me I was adopted once she realized I didn't know. Within under a year of our finally having a conversation about it, Mom was diagnosed with breast cancer.)

Some examples of vows associated with the fourth chakra:

Fourth Chakra/Front of Body	Fourth Chakra/Back of Body
It's better to be alone	*They do not love me*
It's easy for me to love people	*He is not around much*
Love always hurts	*If I eat they won't fight*

Fifth, Communication Chakra

The Sanskrit name of the fifth chakra is Vishuddha, meaning "purification." It is blue and symbolized by a lotus flower with sixteen petals. The fifth chakra regulates the jaw, neck, arms, ears, upper lungs, shoulders, tongue, thyroid, throat, and mouth. It is located at the throat area and its function is using our voice for self-expression and communication. In an unbalanced state we might not be able to communicate in integrity, thoughtfully, or clearly. Vows connected to the communication chakra are related to relationships to others in terms of speaking and listening.

Three examples of disease manifestation at this chakra are:

1. Mouth problems from having set opinions and a closed mind; associated vows are about saying/not saying something the right/wrong way.

2. Shoulder/neck tension due to vows related to speaking the truth, not being allowed to speak the truth, or how someone should or shouldn't talk to you.

3. Jaw issues from anger, resentment, or a desire for revenge; related to vows about keeping one's mouth shut or not talking

back. The constant holding back that one wishes to express often is evidenced by clamping the jaws shut.

Some examples of vows associated with the fifth chakra:

Fifth Chakra/Front of Body	Fifth Chakra/Back of Body
Nobody believes me	*When I'm big enough she won't yell*
I can't say I love her	*He can't talk to me like that*
I cry when he gets loud	*They are not listening*

Sixth, Intuition Chakra

The Sanskrit name of the sixth chakra is Ajna, meaning "perceive" or "beyond wisdom." It is indigo and symbolized by a lotus flower with two petals. The sixth chakra regulates the nose, sinuses, eyes, head, face, and pituitary gland. It is located at the third eye in the center

AJNA

of the forehead, and its function is inner knowing and imagination. In an unbalanced state we might be rigid in our thinking and unable/unwilling to understand something beyond our limited, tunnel vision. Vows connected to the intuition chakra are knowing truth and being understood by others.

Three examples of disease manifestation at this chakra are:

1. Eye problems from not liking what you see; vows related to not seeing or knowing something.

2. Headaches from self-criticism and fear; from most often one of two causative vow groups: I don't/can't/know/know how (to do something); OR doing something (usually repeatedly,

such as a job) that I have vowed is bad (specifically connected to migraine headaches).

3. Nose issues (such as frequent nose bleeds) related to a need for self-recognition.

Some examples of vows associated with the sixth chakra:

Sixth Chakra/Front of Body	Sixth Chakra/Back of Body
When I'm big I can be smart	*She doesn't understand me*
I always have the right answer	*Something is wrong with me*
Girls are not smart	*I have to do it better*

Seventh, Crown Chakra

The Sanskrit name of the seventh chakra is Sahasrara, meaning "thousand" or "infinite." It is violet and symbolized by a lotus flower with 1,000 petals. It is located at the top of the head and its function is spirituality and our connection with the divine. This is the portal through which our life force enters the body. Interestingly, we do not make vows related to spirituality! Any vows

SAHASRARA

related to love expressed at the heart chakra, and any vows about religion (different than spirituality) would involve perceptions about power and communication (such as of the Church) and would be expressed at those respective chakras.

Body Map Vow Tables

There are hundreds of vows that have been discovered over the years with Body Memory Process clients. Keep in mind as you review the vows I've selected as examples in this chapter that when you do the work to discover your own childhood vows, your vows may be the same, similar, or completely different. The diversity of vows is commensurate to the diversity of people.

While most vows will present at one specific chakra, some could impact your body differently, depending upon specifics, and you might need to do more discovery work. As an example, the vow *I am never right enough* will show up differently for each person depending upon *how* you are never right enough. If it's *right* about how I communicate with someone—who tells me I don't communicate clearly, then the throat chakra is involved. If it's about how I show up in the world, and maybe I'm overlooked for promotion, then the power chakra is involved.

Useful Exercises for Integrating What You Learned in This Chapter

1. In the next chapter, you will learn how to discover your own childhood vows and the body map will be a very valuable tool for this process. Begin jotting down notes on anything that especially resonated while reading this chapter.

2. Look online for resources for tuning in to and balancing your chakras. The more you learn about and work with your chakras, the more you will learn about yourself and ease the journey of discovering your childhood vows.

3. Think about the history of pain, tension, or disease in your body through the years. Have issues tended to show up in one side of your body? Take note of which side. Have issues tended to manifest in the front or the back of your body? Take notes with any specific information that you can use in the next steps of your journey!

CHAPTER EIGHT

Discover Your Childhood Vows

You are about to embark on a very exciting part of this journey! Up until now, you have been largely learning about childhood vows through the experiences of Body Memory Process clients. Ultimately, this book is about learning by doing, so you have been completing exercises at the end of each chapter to begin integrating the new
concepts. This has all been preparation for what is to come in this chapter!

At the end of your vow discovery work, you will have discovered many of the vows you created early in life. Whether you will discover all of them is not determined. As you become increasingly more conscious of your inner self and of decoding the clues from your body, you will likely continue to find things to work on throughout your life—like peeling the layers of an onion! During your initial work, you will certainly determine several vows, and by setting a clear intention, you will discover the ones most important to your current life situation.

When David Sohn worked with a client, he would spend the first third of a three-hour session "listening" them. I didn't mean "listening to." David said if you allow someone to talk from a deep level, they will tell you their life script. To "listen" someone means to resist the urge to treat their sharing as a conversation, where you often formulate what you want to say before the other person is finished speaking. This type of engagement increases the risk that you will completely miss something that is said, or not hear the childhood vow lurking beneath their words. For example, someone could say, "I was the middle child, and rarely received enough attention."

The related vow, *nobody ever pays attention to me*, could manifest in adult life as someone who always gets passed over when it's promotion time.

If you are reading this book to work on yourself, you can replicate the opportunity for an objective third-party listener by asking your spouse or a friend to sit down with you and "listen you" as you talk. At this beginning stage, it is about being relaxed and letting whatever is in your conscious mind flow. There will be an opportunity to access valuable subconscious information (from your body) later in the process. Keep in mind that what you are consciously aware of is equally important in your discovery process. Many clients find they enjoy beginning by talking about what has brought them to start working on themselves and then move into talking about their family, life growing up, and whatever else they might be holding in their earliest memories.

If you would prefer to work entirely on your own, you can record yourself talking aloud about what is going on in your life now and also any events from your childhood that you believe are significant. You can then play back the recording, "listen" yourself, and jot down notes on anything you believe is important to this process. If you are reading this book to help someone else, you will have here the tools you need and you will also personally benefit from honing your ability to "listen" someone.

If you would like to do vow discovery work with your children, you can gently encourage them to talk about traumatic experiences that have likely contributed to the formulation of vows. Art and role-playing are good tools for getting kids to open up but know that you might just get a piece at a time. On the other hand, children can be very much open books about their feelings and in this case, you still might just get a piece at a time. Working with them is best done not in a session, but with conscious parenting to catch pertinent information moment-to-moment and day-to-day—which is why keeping a journal for each child is a good idea.

If you are a foster parent or a social worker and have access to a child who has been subjected to severe trauma, you would be doing that child a great service by learning to "listen" them and do what you can to prevent the harmful effects of trauma long into their adulthood.

One of the largest investigations of the connection between adverse childhood experiences (ACE) is a study conducted by the Center for Disease Control and Kaiser Permanente, originally conducted from 1995-1997.[3]

According to the study, children who were greatly subjected to abuse, neglect, and household dysfunction had a significantly elevated risk of adversity in adulthood in the form of severe injuries, depression, anxiety, suicide, unintended pregnancy, cancer, diabetes, alcohol and drug abuse, and lower educational and income opportunities. Also considering the cycle of abuse when a parent doesn't heal their own trauma, you can see the immense importance of doing all we can to help children process and heal trauma.

Your Vow Discovery Process

Please note the following steps in the vow discovery process. This is often an iterative and not linear experience, so feel free to move back and forth between the steps, as needed.

1. MEDITATION—Guided meditation to relax and get into a heightened inner awareness

2. PURPOSE—Review what issues or circumstances bring you to this self-discovery process

3. INTENTION—Set your intention for the session

4. QUESTIONS—Review the entire set of questions and record your answers

5. VOW TYPES/COMMON VOWS—Some of this information you will have seen earlier in the book, but it is pulled together here for easy reference during this process

6. VOWS LISTED BY CHAKRA—This cross-referenced, Excel workbook is available for purchase on the Body Memory Process website at a discounted price for those who have acquired this book.

Meditation

I recommend you choose any recorded guided meditation designed to get you to breathe slowly and deeply and relax you into a state of heightened awareness of your body. Please do not skip the meditation. It will help you recall significant information about your past and present life, and ultimately bring you to a discovery of your childhood vows.

Purpose

Once you have relaxed with your meditation, please review what drew you to this book. Are you experiencing health, financial, relationship, or career challenges? Do you consider yourself to currently be in crisis and are looking for a solution you haven't found anywhere else? Or are you mostly content with your life, but believe you could always experience more joy, more prosperity, and more energy? It is important to have this fresh in your mind as you next move into the intention you will set for your vow discovery session.

Intention

Please next take some time to set your intention for your vow discovery work based on what has brought you here. For example, if you are looking to find your soulmate and are tired of always sabotaging your relationships, connect with whatever you believe in as your higher source and set your intention to discover the childhood vows that have been interfering with your finding a life partner who will deeply understand and support you. You may discover many other, unrelated vows, but setting your clear intention for a primary discovery purpose will ensure these vows will be revealed.

Questions

Next, you will see several questions to assist you with determining your vows. Please note these questions could pull you up from your meditative state. It is important to stay as relaxed and meditative as possible. You will likely need to consult others to help answer some of the questions, so know that it is perfectly fine to pursue that information then return another time to your process, always beginning with a meditation and statement of intention. Please review the summary of chapter five for the main points regarding womb and birth trauma as a part of this process. At the end of each section of questions, you will see a discussion of vow types and common vows to help you determine your own childhood vows.

Questions related to your Conception Experience

1. What do you know about your mother's reaction to learning she was pregnant with you? Was she joyful? Excited? Scared? Upset? Anxious?

2. If you've never heard anything directly from your mother or other family member that will help answer this question, and the information remains unavailable, see what you can infer

about your mother's reaction based on such facts at the time of her pregnancy as her age, her marital status, whether she was still in high school or college, her financial situation, and whether there were already other children in the family.

3.   Was she trying to get pregnant, or did it happen as a surprise?

4.   Did your mother feel she knew the moment she conceived?

5.   Of particular importance is your mother's attitude towards money and whether she felt she had enough to become a mother or have another child. This has very significant implications for your own relationship with money.

Common Conception Vows

Conception vows are easily wired in because the energy at the time is so intense. If you were conceived "accidentally," especially if there was angst from your mother because of it, you could have the vow *I am an accident.* This could bring being accident prone and experienceing bad accidents in life. Consider the importance of the circumstances in this alternative possibility: If you were conceived accidentally and your parents had been perhaps trying to conceive and were ready to quit trying, *I am an accident* could bring an entirely different experience. People with this vow under this circumstance say they can fall into a cesspool and come out smelling like a rose. I'd like to emphasize here that any vow—even seemingly "good vows"—can have negative consequences and should be disavowed. In this example, someone who always escapes accidents unharmed could be resented by those around them. They are also still accident-prone and may grow tired of all the accidents—even with the benign outcomes. Take a moment here to consider if any of this applies to your conception circumstances.

Another conception vow can be *it's all my fault.* This refers to making all the radical changes in Mom and/or Dad's life. This is a vow that I had, and whenever anything around me went south I would cringe, sure that it was either because of something I did or something I didn't do.

There was just no way I could escape feeling guilty until I discovered and disavowed the vow.

Another conception vow can be *sex is bad*. If there is a negative reaction from Mom or Dad to the news of the pregnancy, this vow can be put into place as Mom might have bargained with God that she will never, ever have sex again if she could just get out of this situation. This happens mostly with pregnancies out of wedlock. If you are averse to sex or are inclined to have your sexual experiences be "naughty" or "bad," you could have this vow.

Remember, all vows reinforce themselves as "self-fulfilling prophecies" and will show up throughout life—beginning with life's earliest experiences. So, you may not know anything about your conception but see a vow show up in reviewing your birth experience. Also, remember that it is not important to link a specific vow you find to whether it is conception, womb, birth, or childhood related. Rather, it is by looking through this prism that the vow discovery can more easily occur and that is the extent of its usefulness. What is most important is that you discover your vows so that you can disavow them.

Questions related to your Womb Experience

These questions are designed to elicit whether your womb experience was predominantly feelings of love or feelings of fear or anxiety. Womb vows can come from both positive and negative feelings. Your mother's experience of fear or anxiety—also picked up by the fetus—can be fleeting, but if powerful enough, can result in a very common womb vow, *I'm okay* or *I'm fine*, discussed below.

1. What do you know about your mother's pregnancy with you? Was it easy? Difficult? If difficult, what are the specifics of the difficulty?

2. Did she experience any bumps to her belly or any accidents? Any close calls?

3. Did Mom become ill during her pregnancy? If so, what was the nature of the illness?

4. Do you know if your mother had a previous miscarriage and was therefore particularly anxious about this pregnancy?

5. What were your mother's attitudes about her body changes during her pregnancy?

6. How was her eating? Did she smoke? Drink? Take drugs?

7. We already discussed financial concerns that might have arisen when your mother found out she was pregnant. Did any of those persist and possibly increase during the course of the pregnancy?

8. Was your father present during your mother's pregnancy? There are circumstances that could have resulted in your father being absent, including military assignment, illness, incarceration, and personal choice to be absent—especially if the pregnancy was out of wedlock.

9. If your father was absent during the pregnancy, what was your mother's attitude about that? If your father was present, how engaged was he with the pregnancy? How well did he support your mother?

Common Womb Vows

As a reminder, you could very likely have unique vows that haven't yet been discovered. If you can't find what you believe to be your vow in the list of common vows, this doesn't mean you are wrong—just that you are a unique individual with the potential for a unique set of circumstances and vows!

Very common is a decision in the womb to be just like Mom or just like Dad. This decision is not what we would consider to be the normal process of thinking through something and coming to a conclusion.

This is all about those feelings discussed earlier—either of intense love or intense fear and separation. It occurs on an energetic, feeling level and is about taking on or not taking on the pattern of the adult from whom they are feeling love or separation. When the child acquires language, this opens up the possibility of articulating the vow.

The wording can be *I will be like him, I will be like her, I will be like Mom, I will be like Dad*, or conversely, *will not be...*

I will stress here that the difficulty associated with any vow is its limits on one's ability to choose in the present, adult moment. If I have the vow *I will be like Mom*, I take on both working and non-working behavior patterns. If I have the vow *I will not be like Mom*, not only will I not take on the non-working behavior patterns, but I will also not take on the working behavior patterns!

Another common womb vow—specifically amongst firstborns—is *I am fine*. This is caused by Mom's fear about having a baby for the first time. Usually there is a bump on the belly or something that happens which makes Mom panic. The adrenaline gets passed to the baby, who gets toxic and starts to kick. Mom begs the baby to "be OK," and when Mom calms down there is a connection made that results in the baby deciding his or her own feelings are not as important as Mom's. This vow *I am fine* results in the individual not wanting to talk about their feelings. They can slam their finger in a car door and will still say "I'm OK."

A vow to be either a girl or a boy is very common because the parents often decide what they would prefer while the baby is in the womb and the gender is not yet known. There are a lot of ways the wording of this vow shows up, including *I will be a boy, I will be his boy, I will be your girl, I will be your son, I will be a boy for you*. The result can be enmeshed relationships and girls can become tomboys. If the wording is "boy" instead of "son," there can be difficult growing into a man.

If you don't know anything about your womb experience, whether it was positive or negative, then you can still take time now with these and the hundreds of other vows available in the appendix to see if they resonate.

Questions Related to Your Birth Experience

1. What do you know about your birth? What have you heard from your mother, father, siblings, or any other family member who might have been present or heard stories?

2. Where was your birth? At the hospital? A home birth? An inconvenient location, perhaps on the way to a hospital?

3. Was your birth easy? Difficult? If difficult, what are the specifics of the difficulty?

4. Was your mother given drugs during birth?

5. Were you allowed to be with your mother or were you whisked away to a neonatal intensive care unit?

6. Of particular note regarding the birth experience, do any family members recall what was said during your birth?

Common Birth Vows

A hard, long birth can result in the vow *life is Hard*. The vow *he hurts me* can result from a male doctor performing the immediate after-birth care, including the slap on the bottom or the flick on the feet when doing the Apgar testing. There is a variation *he hurts me and she says it's OK* when Mom is not there to provide immediate comfort.

If the birth team remarks the baby is hurting the mother, there can be *I hurt her* or *I will never hurt her again*. The vow *I hurt her* can be very harmful when it belongs to a male who might end up abusing women. It is strongly suspected that most men who abuse women have an *I hurt her* vow.

The birth vow *something must be wrong with me* can result from any comment by the birth team about something being wrong with the baby—or even after an announcement that "it is a girl" or "it is a boy" if the parents didn't previously know—and there being a brief moment (or longer) of disappointment.

Another common birth vow, *if I don't get out of here, I'm going to die* can occur during a long, complicated birth. Adults with this vow can handle a tremendous amount of stress until they feel constrained and will then have to leave before they "explode."

If you don't know anything about your birth experience, whether it was positive or negative, then you can still take time now with these and the hundreds of other vows available in the appendix to see if they resonate.

Questions Related to Your Family and Childhood

1. Are both of your parents still living? Did any parent die during your childhood?

2. Are your parents still married or are they divorced? Were your parents never married?

3. Which parent supported you the most emotionally?

4. Who did you go to when you wanted to be comforted?

5. Who did you push against?

6. Are you the only child? If not, how many siblings do you have and what were their ages and genders?

7. Are there any significant events you recall from your childhood?

8. Any significant aspects of any relationships with family members, teachers, or other authority figures?

9. Where are you in the birth order?

What I call "infant vows" refer to vows created when children are very young and developing their personalities. Infant vows are most often created from instruction by caregivers, created to obtain love or to feel safe. If an inept or untrained person tells the child "you are bad" often enough, the child will believe the message and construct the vow. If some behavior consistently gets the child love, then the child creates a rule about themselves as a person, their behavior, or the one from which they desire the love.

Vows such as *I will hide* and *I will be quiet* can result from a raging parent and the infant learning that it is safer to hide than to endure more rage. A common infant vow, *I have to be perfect*, often results when education is focused on resisting errors rather than embracing an unfolding that happens at different times for different children. *I am never good enough* can also be the result of the low self-esteem that results from too many put-downs. *I will be a good girl* or *I will be a good boy* is a learned way to get love.

A myriad of ways children are disciplined verbally can result in vows worded similarly to the scolding, such as *I am wrong, I am bad, I never listen,* and even more harsh rebukes such as *I don't deserve to live.* A vow *I will fix it* can come from breaking something or making a mess then fearing the repercussions. This can lead to being a "fixer" in adulthood—always trying to fix situations or other people.

If these common infant vows don't seem to fit you, then you can review the hundreds of other vows available in the appendix to see if they resonate.

Questions Related to Pain and Tension in Your Body

1. Where do you hold recurrent pain and/or tension in your body? Feel through and when you get to the spot, access the adjectives to describe it and write that down.

2. How long have you had this pain/tension? Does it occur regularly? When did it first occur? When does it usually occur?

3. Do you have a physical weakness (such as a trick knee or ankle)? Does it occur regularly? When did it first occur? When does it usually occur?

4. For each of these, be sure to start at your head or your feet and work your way systematically through your entire body.

Here is a special meditative way to interact with what you find in your body, even if you might find it to be a bit silly. It is actually a very powerful way to work with the energy.

First, isolate the tension or pain in your body as accurately as possible. Then imagine the pain moving outside your body as a sphere about three feet in diameter. Next, imagine the sphere in a large pot just big enough to hold the entire sphere as a clear liquid—or any color you choose. If it is a color, you will notice the color is darker and more intense every time you concentrate the liquid. See the liquid being poured out of the large pot into a slightly smaller pot. All of the liquid just barely fits and the pot is full; the liquid is more concentrated. Then pour it into a smaller pot. Once again, the liquid just barely fits and the pot is full; the liquid is more concentrated. This will lead you to concentrate the message.

Focus on the process and repeat it several times until you have the liquid in a one-quart pot. Then see the liquid poured into a clear glass four-cup measuring cup, then into a two-cup measuring cup, then a one-cup measuring cup. Finally, pour it into a small clear glass. You want to listen to the message in this concentrated form. As you look at the liquid in the glass, you notice it has eyes and a mouth. Now you ask the liquid, "If you had a message for me what would it be? What do you want to say to me?"

Allow yourself to be open to whatever the message is from your pain. Then, you can ask clarifying questions and understand the decisions you made which are causing the pain. When you are sure you have the information you desire, always be sure to ask the pain, "Is there anything else you want to say to me?"

Through this process you can detect the wording of your related childhood vows and you can also review the hundreds of vows available in the appendix to check for what might resonate.

In addition to where you hold pain and tension in your body, many clues about your childhood vows can be reflected in your current adult life in the areas of finances, relationships, and career. Please take the time to write down all the details that you can recall about these areas of your life then review the vows in the appendix for what might resonate.

This is the end of the vow discovery process. If you are satisfied with the list of vows you have discovered, you are ready to go on to the next chapter for the homework for vow release. If you are not satisfied that you have revealed the vows you are seeking, take a deep breath, relax, and go through the process again. In the over thirty years of working with Body Memory Process clients, we have never seen a client walk away empty-handed. Don't try to force anything—just be meditative with the information and know that what you need to work on will be revealed to you.

CHAPTER NINE

Release Your Childhood Vows

One day in a Tibetan monastery, a man who had recently arrived sat down for tea with a great teacher. As the monk picked up the teapot, the student said, "Master, I have studied with many wise ones the world over and I already know a lot. In fact, I probably don't even need to be here, but I heard you were one of the greatest teachers in this land, so I came to find you."

As the master teacher began to pour the tea, the man continued, "I want you to teach me all you know. Share with me your great wisdom!"

The master teacher continued to pour the tea until it overflowed the cup and onto the table.

The man looked up in surprise and said, "Master, please stop pouring, my cup is full!"

The master teacher looked him in the eyes and said, "So is your mind. I cannot teach you anything," after which he put the teapot down and left the room.

It may seem extremely obvious but is worth stating here, because it is so important to the healing process, that if something is full, nothing else can be added. It all comes down to the law of physics that two objects cannot occupy the same space! The man who visited Tibet expressed the desire for more knowledge and wisdom but was more invested in what he already knew than what he didn't know. The master teacher knew that anything he tried to teach the man would be compared to something he thought he already knew. This is why it is vital for a student to approach any new topic with a clear and open mind.

Computers have given us another opportunity to learn this lesson. In the days of floppy disks, when you went to save a file but there wasn't enough room on the disk you would receive an error message that was something like "disk is full, try again." Now, you could say the unstated assumption was that you should free up disk space and then try again—but as the statement was written, it was an exercise in futility!

The underlying premise of the Body Memory Process homework is the need to "empty the cup" of the cell memory so that the childhood vows can be released to allow you to create what you want as an adult. In chapter one, we discussed Dr. Candace Pert, whose research proved that traumatic emotional events are reflected in the body. These deep roots manifest within the cells of the body's organs, glands, and muscles and will perpetually update each new cell with the information—unless and until the spiritual being in that body decides to consciously intervene.

The Body Memory Process homework process you will learn in this chapter is unique in its approach to "emptying the cup" physically, mentally, and emotionally. There are other methods available to deal with the blocked energy, such as various forms of energy work, but the relief will be only temporarily if the belief is still encoded in the cell.

How many of us have tried willpower to make lasting change? If you have ever written a list of new year's resolutions, you are probably familiar with this classic battle between the mind and the body and it might look something like this: I want to begin going to the gym but  because I work a day job, I will need to go either before or after work. The first day the alarm clock goes off at 5:00 a.m. I hit the snooze a couple of times and miss my window of opportunity. Or perhaps I successfully hit the gym for a few days but then start noticing I miss the extra hour of sleep and derail there. If I decide to go after work then I have to deal with all the other things I would do with that time, such as relaxing on the couch watching a show or playing a game. If my willpower is strong, I might be motivated enough to forego all the other options. Eventually, however, there is a good chance I'll start missing my usual after-work relaxation time and will give in to old habits.

Whether I tried to work out in the morning or the afternoon, I was up against a powerful force of opposition—my habits! In the morning, I was in the habit of sleeping until 6:00 a.m. In the afternoon, I was in the habit of flopping onto the couch for some pre-dinner relaxation. All of my habits are encoded in my body memory and trying to use my brain, or willpower alone, is much like trying to push a chain.

In much the same way, my beliefs—and how I act in accordance with those beliefs—are encoded in my cellular memory and shows up in my life as a habit. Earlier, we saw many examples of clients who were in the habit of sabotaging relationships, being overly concerned about appearances, expecting family fights, and "snatching defeat from the jaws of victory." The only way they were able to end those habits was by creating a new habit called the Body Memory Process homework, which has a vow release process that lasts ninety days—about how long it takes to train cellular memory into a new habit.

The Body Memory Process homework to release your childhood vows is comprised of the disavowal process—which empties the physical cup, the affirmation process—which empties the mental cup, and the forgiveness process—which empties the spiritual cup.

The Disavowal Process

At least twice a day for ninety days, take time to relax, then declare each disavowal in turn, allowing time after each one for the body energy to shift and then settle down. A disavowal is formed by saying "I disavow . . ." in front of each vow you have discovered. It is necessary to notice the energy in the body and such brain tricks as "I disavow *that*..." Do not insert "that" after "I disavow . . ." because it shifts the process from your body to your brain. I usually say my disavowals with strong intention and some emotion, as emotion was key to putting in the belief in the first place. For example, when I disavowed *they watch me to see when I am going to die* I would say, *I disavow they watch me to see when I am going to die* with strong conviction in my voice that this belief no longer served me and I was ready to let it go!

When you notice pain or tension associated with a specific disavowal, declare the disavowal and notice the pain or tension lessen or often disappear altogether. This part of the process allows you to notice the body and respond to it more, thus assisting in ease of communication with the cellular memory. Noticing behavior associated with a specific disavowal, then declaring that disavowal, often eliminates the unconscious urge to act in a certain way. It is then possible to choose a new behavior rather than reinforcing old, non-supportive vows.

You might find yourself wondering why this works. There is a 21/90 rule that states that it takes twenty-one days to form a habit and ninety days to make a lifestyle change. By utilizing the principles discovered by sports trainers regarding the use of repetitive instruction to retrain the body, it is possible to alter body memory about anything. The sports coach knows it takes three months to train an athlete a new way. They even say that at three months "if he hasn't gotten it by now, he won't get. . ." whatever the desired result happens to be.

At about the sixth week of the process of changing the cellular memory, a shift occurs and one notices the disavowals seem to have only a small portion of their previous effect. This occurs because you have reached the point when a greater number of cells in any given area have the new information than those retaining the old.

Many people are tempted to discontinue their repetitive work at this point and, in theory, the cells should over a period of time teach all the new cells the new information. However, I recommend continuing the repetitive work until the full three months have elapsed. This seems to accelerate the healing process and more readily assures you of obtaining the full benefit of doing this work.

Remember, if you pick and choose which vows to work on, your results will reflect this. I had a client who did none of the homework on his health-related vows because he deeply did not believe we can change our health. He did, however, do the work on his prosperity issues and saw a great improvement in his finances. He subsequently decided the work was perhaps powerful enough to work on health issues too!

Children can do the Disavowal Process, or you can say "I [child's name] disavow [vow]" for each vow you've discovered, following the adult process. I have a son on the autism spectrum who didn't talk until he was six years old and I did several disavowals for him as "I Benjamin disavow . . ." until he began talking and could say the disavowals for any new vows we discovered.

Forgiveness Process

The purpose of forgiveness is to give up the right or desire to punish or change someone. The following forgiveness process is based on the seven (days) X seventy formula provided in the Holy Bible, and which has also been used with much success for over thirty years with Body Memory Process clients. You can split this in half—twenty minutes in the morning and twenty minutes in the evening, or do your forgiveness for the day in one session.

On each of seven days in a row, on a clean page in your notebook, number one through seventy, skipping every other line. Write the following sentence seventy times: "I, [your name], forgive [a person you blame] totally and unconditionally." If you do this in two sessions, you will write thirty-five sentences at a time. If you skip a day, this will indicate resistance to the process, and you will need to take a deep breath and begin the process again. When the seven days are completed, burn the paper as this will purify the energy.

It is important to teach children to forgive (especially through enjoyable stories about animals), but they should never be forced to forgive until they are ready.

Who should you forgive? It is necessary to forgive all the significant players in your life. This list includes *but is not limited to* the following:

- Birth Team—those in attendance at your birth. These people are the first group of authority figures you meet
- Mom (or the name you used for her)
- Dad (or the name you used for him)
- Siblings (each, individually by name)
- Significant adults (by the name you called them) who had a strong influence on you
- Partners (each by name)
- Children (each by name)
- God
- Yourself

The following is an amusing account of a client who noticed his resistance to the forgiveness process but kept pushing on anyway!

> *The first day I started work on her it was just difficult to finish seventy lines of "I Joe forgive Margaret." I didn't really want to even spend that much energy on her. I kept reminding myself that I might as well forgive her because she wasn't worth spending the energy required to be mad. I eventually made it through the first day, hands aching and mind recalling. I was just happy I had done it.*
>
> *By the second day I had a little easier time of it. I wasn't constantly asking myself why I was doing it—I just did it because it needed to be done. "Forgive, forgive, forgive" kept going through my head. I had to stop several times to let my hand recover.*
>
> *On the third day, Margaret sought me out and did her best to lay all her troubles on my sympathetic ears, only they weren't sympathetic.*

I rushed home after listening to her and thought, "To forgive is divine."

Breathe. . .Relax. . . Of course, Jesus never met Margaret! No, relax . . . I balled up all the energy I wanted to use to rip her head off and grounded it so I could do my forgiveness work for that day. This day was a struggle because I didn't want to focus on her while I was writing. My mind kept wandering to upcoming papers, meetings, etc. . . I spent a lot of time refocusing on Margaret so I could get it done right.

By the fourth day I didn't want to kill her anymore. "Ah, progress," I thought.

I noted how difficult it was to do the forgiveness work with somebody constantly present in my life, reminding me why I needed to forgive them. Yes, she annoyed me on a daily basis, but I knew if I could just get through those seven days of forgiveness, I would have moved the energy required to see her as a human being again. I plodded ahead.

My hands weren't hurting as much by the fifth day of my forgiveness work. I've noticed that they usually don't by the fifth day. The breakthrough I was striving for was close at hand and my energy grounded enough to move through the anger I felt.

Each sentence became increasingly more difficult on the sixth day. As I approached acceptance of forgiving Margaret, my body wasn't sure it wanted to let go of this pattern. I was stopping every three or four sentences to recompose myself. Actually, my hands are beginning to hurt now, just recalling the process!

By the seventh day I was so happy that I had made it I was almost elated that my hand hurt as much as it did. I moved to a place of forgiving her, especially for the delight I was taking from this process. It was painstaking, this final day. Mulling over every minute detail of her habits, dysfunctional perceptions and relations, my mind painted a clear picture of why I needed to forgive this person. This was all her stuff, not mine. I don't want to take it on, and by forgiving her I could let it go. Focus, forgive, focus, forgive . . . I made it.

What will happen when I forgive her again? Well, I expect to not jump every time she wants to talk to me. The first day or two will be *relatively easy and, as I remember why it's important to forgive her, it will probably get harder to write. Still, I expect that by the seventh day I will have a hand that hurts and an excited elation regarding this momentous work. And she will remind me of this gift every time I see her.*

The Affirmation Process

An affirmation is a tool to assist in clearing negative self-messages. We are told to state positive affirmations, but often when we do, we hear our brain chatter all the reasons that statement isn't true! This process is designed to give your brain the chance to "talk." Remember, the brain doesn't like change, because change can threaten your safety. It is important to not let your brain be in charge of your life. This process allows you to address your brain's concerns and ultimately be clear that this is a change that you want and that is good for you.

Write the affirmation on the left page and then write all of the brain's responses on the right page. It is often possible to write a full page of responses while only writing the affirmation a few times.

After the response page is full, burn it. It is important to note that burning the affirmation response page purifies the energy. Do this process as often as you like, for the more you work with it, the sooner you will achieve the desired results.

Sample Affirmations to Explore

- ✦ *I am the one they want/chose* (conception)
- ✦ *I am perfect just the way I am* (womb experience or low self-esteem; all the "wrong with me" beliefs)
- ✦ *People love me just the way I am* (accidental conception/womb/birth experience/unwanted—especially if low self-esteem)
- ✦ *I am alive/I am joyfully alive* (birth—especially if Mom was drugged)

+ *I am the right one* (parents wanted opposite sex child)

+ *Life is safe* (troubled pregnancy; mother contemplated or attempted abortion; abuse in infancy)

+ *Now is the right/perfect time* ("late" or premature birth)

+ *My timing is perfect* ("fast" or "slow" birth)

+ *Life is easy* (hard birth or constant struggle)

+ *I am whole and/or complete* (scarcity beliefs, money problems)

The Affirmation Process is mainly for adults who have a lot of brain chatter, but children should also be encouraged to make affirmative statements, then discuss with them how their body feels when they make the statement—and if they have any associated thoughts. What works best for children is instead of a written process, make the affirmation a fun process to talk through together. If you are caring for a child who has been severely traumatized, the following are some effective affirmations to work on together:

+ I am safe

+ I am loved

+ I am wanted

+ I am perfect just the way I am

You can also take the vows you've discovered with the child and reword them affirmatively. An example is a vow *there is never a right place for me* and the affirmation *I am always in the right place for me.*

The following is an account of a client who had some brain interference to her affirmation process!

> *My process of doing affirmations worked great until I came across one strongly held by my inner child: School is easy for me. For the first couple of days, memories from my childhood came out and things I didn't even remember consciously appeared as if out of nowhere. After the first night, I had an interesting combination of frustration and relief.*

Part of me was upset by the memories that were brought up (I had no idea this belief of being stupid was buried so deep), while another part of me was relieved that they were finally coming out into the open to be healed. After the memories, my brain began to spit up past experiences that would back-up my false belief.

Then, finally, there came some positive reinforcement! My brain began to support me in my thoughts of being intelligent, but after a while of this it began to ramble about anything other than school is easy for me. My brain was obviously not interested in fully dispelling this belief. Noticing that I did not remain focused when doing the affirmation, I called my coach, who advised me to use a more powerful way to do the affirmation. I was told to write down the affirmation and then whatever came to mind. If nothing came to mind, then that's what I was to write and to continue this process repeatedly.

My brain was resistant to finishing this process. It did not want me to get to the real heart of the issue. My brain wanted to remain in control; that is the reason it began to wander. With this new information, I sat down again, and after ten or fifteen minutes of writing the affirmation then "nothing," the heart of the matter finally appeared. I am capable of getting an "A" in chemistry, but I do not want to. I am satisfied with passing the class; I just don't want to get an "A."

My resistance to chemistry had been in believing that I had to get an "A" to prove I am intelligent. I know I am intelligent and getting an "A" does not prove this. I see now that I also believed that I needed to get an "A" to satisfy others, not myself. My breakthrough is not only in finding the reason why I have made chemistry so hard; it is also in this affirmation process.

As you look through your list of vows that you discovered during your vow discovery process, know that you can work on all of them at one time, regardless of how many there are, as it does not take long to say them. I like to say each of mine twice just to be sure I have the opportunity really be with each one for those few seconds.

You can use your vows as a guide for who to forgive. In my case, I chose to forgive my birth mother as a priority. You can also work with your vows to find the best affirmations to do to complement the disavowal work. For example, one of my affirmations to accompany my disavowal work on *they watch me to see when I am going to die,* was *I am alive, strong, and speak my truth with conviction and confidence.* Yes, I had a lot of brain chatter to deal with at first about all those knee-knocking moments of terror in front of a group. But I kept working with it until I no longer heard the "yes, but what about the time. . ." coming from my brain!

PART III

CONSCIOUS LIVING AND WELLNESS

CHAPTER TEN

Consciously Commit to Wellness

During or after reading this book, you will have done something amazing that most people haven't yet accomplished. You will become consciously aware of the unconscious commitments you've been carrying around since childhood. There will likely be more you will discover as time goes on, for self-discovery—as mentioned earlier—is like peeling an onion. Still, most people initially discover a major portion of non-working beliefs that have been reflected in their world.

In *You Can Heal Your Life*, Louise Hay wrote, "All the events you have experienced in your lifetime, up to this moment, have been created by your thoughts and beliefs you have held in the past. They were created by the thoughts and words you used yesterday, last week, last month, last year, ten, twenty, thirty, forty or more years ago, depending on how old you are. However, that is in your past. It is over and done with. What is important in this moment is what you are choosing to think and say now."[4]

I would like you to take a few moments to think about this phenomenal step in your unfoldment—and no matter what your age, to consider everything that has happened to you up until now to be the first chapter of your life's story. More senior readers might think your life up until now has a lot more chapters than one, but I urge you to think of non-working behavior in terms of "before conscious" (BC)! For many of you, this isn't the first book you've read in order to help you learn about yourself, but I would dare to surmise that the self-discovery work contained herein is at a much deeper level than you have previously experienced.

So, I have two questions for you: What will you do with the first chapter of your life? And what will you create once you are conscious and free of most of your non-working thoughts and beliefs? First, let's consider the value of your BC story and the powerful impact you can have by being willing to share to inspire others. I offer my own story as an example, some of which you read during the introduction to this book.

My life began with an unexpected attack from my birth mother, who attempted an abortion at home near the end of her second trimester. For much of my life, I would become highly distraught whenever I experienced an unexpected attack—such as a sudden, explosive argument coming from someone I loved. Communication and relationships were confusing and difficult for me until I began to trust my intuition and allow what would be a deep and profound healing to set me on a new, much happier path. Ultimately, I have become what I refer to as a "wounded healer"—someone who can help others heal and find peace through my own wounding and rise from the ashes.

Now, when I have the opportunity to write about my own "first chapter," I focus on the choices I made (some conscious, many driven by unconscious beliefs) and on forgiveness. I have forgiven David for leaving me to raise our young children alone, knowing he is always by my side. I have forgiven my birth mother because she did the best that she could with what she had at the time. She gave me the tremendous gifts of strength and tenacity that have served me well through the years and will continue to do so. I have also forgiven my over-protective adoptive mother and thank her for teaching me the importance of trusting my own intuition, finding my own voice, and not being afraid to tell what I know to be truth.

The inclination for many people is to beat themselves up once they become more conscious. They think of all the "wasted time" they have spent going around in circles, avoiding opportunities, hiding from

CONSCIOUSLY COMMIT TO WELLNESS   123

the truth, and living in fear instead of love. Please, please do not beat yourself up. Instead, be joyful that you have awakened while there is still time to set upon a purposeful journey, embrace new opportunities, shout the truth, and live in a place of love, not fear!

We live in a time when opportunities and tools are continually emerging that allow anyone to tell their story to help inspire, encourage, and motivate others. Social media has allowed for some deep and moving stories to be told, but it is also largely inundated with superficial exchanges that promote unconscious behavior. We will discuss storytelling and outreach some more in the concluding chapter of this book.

Once you have done the Body Memory Process homework, you are essentially a clean slate—not because there isn't more onion to peel back, but because you now hold the chalk in your adult hand, guided by your now-logical mind and your open, loving heart. You might think of this clean slate as a state of chaos—as discussed in chapter three. If you will recall, an artist staring at a blank canvas holding his palette is in chaos until he organizes the image he wants to convey. Metaphorically holding the chalk to your clean slate is embracing change to create your life, *now consciously*.

Let us consider some behaviors of wellness which I encourage you to incorporate into your life now that you are more fully aware of the power of conscious living.

Physical Wellness

Now is the time to revisit the concepts from chapter one about listening to your body. Remember, your body always gives you cues to when you are hungry, full, thirsty, tired, need the bathroom, and need to move or stretch. It also gives you feedback on your eating, water consumption, and sleep and exercise habits. Now that you are living consciously, be sure to pay attention to your body's cues and feedback. When you have been heeding the basic signals for a while, you might start noticing more specific messages. For example, you might start craving a certain food that contains nutrition that is missing from your diet or stretches that are best for energizing you in the morning versus those that are best for soothing and relaxing your body after a busy day.

It is also important to ensure that for the majority of the time, you are eating unprocessed, non-GMO food and choosing fresh organic meats, fruits, and vegetables. Be sure to drink water that is filtered for impurities. Be a label reader in the supermarket and check for sodium content and unhealthy ingredients like high fructose corn syrup.

Mental Wellness

Now that you are aware that your thoughts, words, and beliefs shaped your reality when you were very young—and perhaps some of the results didn't work well in your life—you will want to be sure to consciously steward your thoughts, words, and beliefs. Do not, however, become distraught if you catch yourself thinking negatively or if self-limiting words come out of your mouth. One thing that you can do for immediate damage control is say "cancel, cancel, cancel" right away. You will find that you will cultivate an observer part of yourself and increasingly catch yourself in the act of being unconscious. Please know that this is a part of living consciously! All that matters is that you have the realization and can then make an adjustment, being gentle with yourself.

It is akin to losing weight and then being on a maintenance program, which is really about having a new lifestyle that is driven by conscious eating. Does being on a maintenance program mean you deprive yourself of all the goodies you still crave? No. It means being aware of your choices and following up with any needed adjustments be sure you stay on track—maintaining the lifestyle that gets you the results you want.

I used to have a teacher who said, "It's not the birds that fly over your head that you need to worry about. It's the ones that make a nest in your hair!"

This means a limiting thought isn't going to ruin your new conscious lifestyle. What will derail you is getting caught up in an illusion—mentally and emotionally.

Emotional Wellness

In chapter two you learned that children create vows from experiences that involve both negative and positive emotions. The same creative power endowed upon us that children use to create vows is the creative power you currently hold consciously within you. The only difference is now you are logical, educated by  life's experiences, and aware of what you are wielding when you engage your mind and your emotions. If you get caught up in a limited idea, an illusion that immerses you in fear instead of love, despair instead of knowing, and sadness instead of joy, you will be at risk of creating a result for yourself that you might not want. If you fearfully put more faith in disease than in your own power to create sustained health, you are at risk of creating illness for yourself. If you invest more despair over your debts than knowing that you can attract the money you require to be debt-free and much more, then you are at risk of missing the opportunity to be prosperous. If you invest more energy in being sad that you don't have a working relationship than in being happy that the perfect-for-you partner is out there, then you are at risk of missing the opportunity to find your soulmate.

Environmental Wellness

When you begin clean living and paying attention to what you consume by reading labels at the grocery store, you will find yourself suddenly aware of the ingredients in many other items in your home that you use every day. Makeup, toothpaste, soap, shampoo, conditioner, hair spray, lotions, creams, air fresheners, laundry detergent, dishwasher detergent, and cleaning supplies can all contain ingredients that are harmful. There are many resources available online to read to become more aware of hazards and to make informed, conscious choices to protect yourself and your family.

Attitudinal Wellness

I like to remember five ways I can be happy every single day, no matter what is going on in my life. First, before getting out of bed in the morning, I count my blessings. What you focus on, you create. If you worry and think about what you don't have, you'll create more need. By thinking about what you *do* have, you create more abundance in your life! To further put yourself in a positive frame of mind for the day, focus on what you plan to do and how it aligns with your values. Thought leader Charles Fillmore used to say this first thing in the morning: "I fairly sizzle with zeal and spring forth to do the things today that ought to be done by me."

Secondly, review your purpose, or what David Sohn would call your "stand" in life. This is your calling, or what Joseph Campbell called "your bliss." If you feel trapped in a job that doesn't truly align with your values and you don't want to jump out of bed and get started every day, it might be time to seriously think about making a change.

Thirdly, don't distinguish between work and play! Start thinking of everything as play. I once had a supervisor who would walk around the office on Mondays and loudly say, "Thank God it's Monday!" because he was trying to counter the pervasive mentality that says the weekends are fun and weekdays aren't. I used to think housework was drudgery until I began putting on music and making it a party.

Fourthly, always look for opportunities to do random acts of kindness. When you reach out and make someone else's day easier and happier, it's going to make you happy. It often takes just a small effort on your part to make a huge difference in someone else's life.

Fifthly, don't get derailed if something goes wrong! We've all heard people answer the question about how they are doing today by answering, "I'm having a bad day!" Chances are, something minor but irritating happened, like they got caught in a traffic jam or had to run back into the house for their keys, then back for their phone (speaking from experience). Remember we discussed earlier that children tend to exaggerate with "always" and "never?" One way to become aware that you are back in a pre-logical child mentality is to realize you have taken a bad moment and exaggerated it into a "bad day." The danger here is that you *could* create a bad day by your focus being on what went wrong instead of your values and your purpose.

Spiritual Wellness

Spiritual wellness is not about going to church or even saying your prayers every morning or before you go to bed at night. Going to church every Sunday or obligatory prayer can become rote, and we all know how habits lend themselves to unconscious behavior. This is not to say religion doesn't serve a valuable purpose. I went to twelve years of Catholic school and I consider those years to be foundational to my strong connection to the Divine. Religious belief and spirituality are different for everyone and it is not my place to advise that your relationship with the Divine be a certain way. What I would like to share with you is the joy I have found in consciously being spiritual as an everyday and "in the moment" experience. When I see a beautiful sunset, receive an unexpected compliment, money, opportunity, or gift, and feel the love of my family and pets, I think of my Divine source and am thankful. Prayer for me is mostly spontaneous, although I will admit I have a prayer that I say with the children every day as we drive off to school. It is a prayer that acknowledges each day that the Divine is in charge, we are safe, we have fun, we learn, and we grow.

In addition to an attitude of gratitude, I make forgiveness an important part of my life. We have seen how powerful forgiveness is in healing from the past. It is also a powerful relationship tool in day-to-day life when breakdowns can occur. It is easy to become indignant if someone yells at you or if a misunderstanding leaves you feeling hurt and confused. This is the time to reach out to the others involved, not withdraw.

Everything in life is made up of energy and everything carries a certain vibration. Negative emotions and experiences can lower our vibration, leaving us more vulnerable to anything that matches lower vibration such as illness, accidents, and crime. If you meditate on this to understand it at an increasingly deep level, you will naturally begin do what is needed to raise your vibration as much as possible. This will include putting new habits in place to daily meditate, pray, forgive, be thankful, and be joyful.

CHAPTER ELEVEN

Conscious Parenting

Whether you are a parent now, want to be in the future, or are not interested in being a parent, this chapter is for you. Those readers who are not interested in parenting a child might still interact with children as an aunt, uncle, teacher, church leader, librarian, or scout leader. The information in this chapter is written primarily for those who interact deeply and daily with children, but the awareness-building is still pertinent to those who interact with kids, even briefly.

You never know the impact you can make on a young mind and heart. I heard a teacher recently talking on a podcast about how many elementary school children she taught mentioned her as a major influence when they were recognized for an honor upon graduation from high school. I remember a scout leader telling me I was going to be a leader one day—and she wasn't talking about just scouting. Did I believe her? Heck, no! I was an insecure young teenager who thought she must have me confused with someone else. Still, I've never forgotten what my scout leader told me and it's one of the clearest memories of my youth.

Each parent desires to make their children's lives better than how they perceive their own. The best way to do this has nothing to do with money and social status. It has everything to do with ensuring we don't pass our unresolved issues to our children and teaching them early on to have life lessons be easy. The foremost gift a parent can bestow is the opportunity for their children to create a life that works by allowing them to observe working patterns in their parents. This means the best way to ensure a better life for your child is creating a better life for yourself—now—no matter what has happened in the past. Furthermore, a strong relationship between the parents is paramount to the balanced development of the child.

Let's look at the child's earliest developmental stages and the impact of parental thoughts and actions. First, there is conception. A conscious conception is the "cleanest" for the child and gives him the smallest amount of material on which to base vows. The embryonic child should never be thought of as an "accident," even when the parents are surprised by the result of their activity. Further, the child is never the "cause of the changes" made by the family which are, in truth, being made due to the parents' desire to have a child. As you probably have noticed by now, parents simply create the best environment when they are conscious and responsible.

Time in the womb is an opportunity to begin to create a strong, loving bond between the parents and the baby. It is also a time when the fetal child is at risk of making self and life commitments based on parental expectations. Hopes regarding the baby can be for a girl or a boy, the "perfect child," "a gift from God," the "last hope" for Mom and Dad's relationship, an athlete, or a genius. While these desires are understandable, there is overwhelming evidence from Body Memory Process clients that there is a connection between the expectations of the parent while the baby is in the womb and related issues that show up for the child later in life.

A conscious communication of love and the directing of positive thoughts to the infant every day is invaluable in creating a clear space for him or her. This is the reason that anyone choosing to be a parent would best integrate a meditation practice into their daily life. Meditation creates the opportunity to balance momentary thoughts and fears, experienced by every normal person regarding parenting, with self-love, confidence, and love for the emerging life.

The objective during the infant's womb experience is for the mother to be in a balanced state and for the father to support that state. It

is, however, unreasonable to think there
is any possibility of a pregnancy being
without stressful moments. Unresolved
issues for the parents will inevitably erupt
time and again in the form of internal
worry and arguments with each other.
If the parents are doing their best to be
conscious but have a brief argument about
money, for example, it would be ideal for
Mom and Dad to reassure the child that
the argument was momentary and declare
out loud the Universal Law, "There is always enough for me."

Otherwise, the baby is at risk of feeling Mom's turmoil and vow to
"never be any trouble," "not need much," or "take care of myself."

I once had a conscious mother explain to me her own method
of cultivating awareness about her impact on her developing child.
She imagined she had a recording device that was capable of playing
back every feeling she experienced for nine months of gestation to
play years later as a life script. She said she thought every day about
that recording being as positive as possible. Many women who are
anxious for their pregnancy to end inadvertently communicate to
the child messages about their discomfort and the inconvenience of
being pregnant.

In summary, the womb experience is best when free of parental
expectation, desire, and stress. The woman's body knows this so
completely that, as science has proven, one of the ways for an infertile
woman to become fertile is to reduce the stress in her life.

Conscious adults, properly prepared for the birth of a child, are the
only ones who should be at the birth. The newborn child is eager to know,
love, and record every word spoken during the birth process. Dr. Leboyer
states in *Birth Without Violence* the importance of awareness on the part
of the adults present at birth: " . . . we must prepare ourselves for this.
We must be awake and aware. Aware that the baby can hear, aware of

how sensitive its hearing is, and how easily harmed. In brief, we must all learn in this first moment to love the baby for itself. Not for ourselves."[5]

Now consider the conscious, baby-oriented birth. The room temperature is high, extremely warm compared to an adult comfort level, and it is very dimly lit. No one speaks except to give support to the mother. Perhaps there 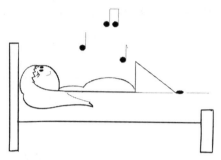 is music the baby has heard in the womb softly playing. The mother, understanding and prepared for the process, is not alarmed or experiencing intense pain as she realizes that the stretching is a natural part of the process which she has practiced daily in birthing relaxation meditations. Drugs are not necessary. There is no emergency, no life-saving distress. The baby, when born, is placed on top of Mom to feel the familiar heartbeat. After a transition time from being immersed in fluid to being surrounded by air, the blood in the placenta will be absorbed into the baby's body. Then and only then the umbilical cord is cut, after which the baby is cleaned by Mom and Dad with the assistance of others. Most babies are relaxed and many even smile during this type of birth—far different from the screams of pain in the delivery room and the plaintive cries in the hospital nursery, associated with an unconscious birth.

While not always the best child-centered practice, doctors do the best they can and it serves no purpose to blame them for problems resulting from unconscious birthing—any more than it does to blame one's parents. Dr. Verny states this in *The Secret Life of the Unborn Child:* " . . . as is so often the case in medicine, we learn how and why things go right by first understanding how they go wrong."[6] Conscious parenting is simply a moment-to-moment choice by the parents to be conscious. It begins with approaching simple tasks such as feeding, bathing, and changing diapers as a loving process rather than as a troublesome, interfering task. This is but one way to express love to the infant. What message is given to the child when changing a soiled diaper is approached by the parent with disgust or an attitude of repulsion?

One friend of mine said her son had trouble eating. My reply was, "What if you consider that you might have trouble feeding him?"

She told me weeks later she had changed her approach to mealtime and the problems had all but disappeared. She said she decided nothing was more important at mealtime than feeding her son and, surprisingly to her, he decided to eat with full attention. A simple (but not necessarily easy) solution was for the mother to approach the task with the same level of commitment she desired in her child. She told me the big breakthrough happened one day when the phone rang at dinner time, and she allowed her focus to remain on his dinner. She said, "He relaxed when I said that if it was important, they would call back, and then he accepted another spoonful of peas."

This simple act creates the space of "You are more important to me than _____ (i.e., the telephone)" in the relationship. The impact will last a lifetime, facilitating communication during the most difficult growth periods of the child.

David Sohn said that when he was learning to teach, one of his own teachers taught him that teaching is simple—you just have to regard the subject as brand new and discover it as you go along. A child, given a crayon, makes marks. A conscious parent, thinking for a child, teaches that marks are best made on paper and does not blame, berate, or beat the child if the marks appear on a wall. While shame and whipping do create behavior changes, they also teach the child that an unmarked wall is more important than he is.

In childhood, we reinforce the vows we made at conception, during our womb experience, and at birth. Then we add to the list more vows which we believe keep us safe and get us the love we desire. As we have discussed earlier, many childhood vows are "have to" statements such as *I have to do it myself*. A conscious approach for the parents is to encourage the desire for independence by facilitating the idea, *I want to do it for myself.* Instead of telling a child, "You have to brush your teeth," it would be better to say, "You want to brush your teeth instead of me doing it for you."

One friend told me of teaching his son to brush his teeth, an event the son regarded as an unwelcome chore. He told me his wife had become frustrated and had given up. My friend said that he just didn't say anything to his son about brushing his teeth for about three days, after which he approached him, asked him to run his tongue over his teeth, then asked him to go brush his teeth, which he supervised. Then he again asked his son to run his tongue over his teeth and said, "Any time you want to stop the furry teeth feeling, go brush! I recommend every morning and evening."[7]

A child does *not* need a village to raise him, as a village is full of diverse and often conflicting messages. A child *does* need conscious parents. We are all familiar with the child who learns they can play one parent against another, so it is critical for a mother and father to not project two different sets of rules for life. This means transcending disagreements and acting as a team. In *The Emotional Incest Syndrome*, the authors state, "It is important . . . that [parents] publicly support each other. Whenever possible, they negotiate behind the scenes and present a united front to their children. When that is not possible, they support each other's decisions . . ." A conscious parent can observe their child and notice vows he has already made. They can gently assist the child in a re-examination of the information that led to the vow and can then be in the position to release the vows for the child. One phenomenal example of this was presented to me by my friend whom I'll call "Nancy." Nancy had four children, the eldest in college when she and her husband "Joe" were surprised to discover that Nancy was pregnant. Joe and Nancy were aligned throughout the pregnancy with Nancy's choice to stop working in order to have a healthy pregnancy, although this choice created many changes for the family. Karen was born naturally, happy, and healthy, and the entire family was excited about the new addition. Karen had one very disturbing pattern, though. Every time Nancy's mother "Doris" held her, Karen would scream and struggle as violently as a newborn could. Nancy began thinking about her mother and conversations they had during the first few weeks of her pregnancy. After becoming suspicious, Nancy visited her mother alone. During their conversation, Nancy bluntly asked Doris if she had thought she should abort the pregnancy. Doris admitted she had, right until the first time she saw Karen. They discussed all the fear Doris experienced during Nancy's pregnancy, and Nancy returned home having chosen to correct this vow for her daughter. Each day for the next week she told Karen about Doris's love for both Nancy and Karen and explained that Doris had just been afraid. Doris visited the following weekend and Nancy reported later to me, "I was astounded in the change in Karen."

She told me Karen had been only slightly uncomfortable in her grandmother's arms. Over the next several weeks, Nancy continued the healing process "from time to time." Soon afterward, Nancy reported that she was encountering a new problem: "My mother is spoiling Karen rotten!"

Conscious parenting may seem like a lot of work because it is so much easier to interact with our children the way our parents did with us. You will find your efforts rewarding, however, not only with regard to your relationship with your children, but with what life brings you when you live consciously. You cannot be a conscious parent without being conscious about everything discussed in the previous chapter.

In conclusion, the conscious parent gift keeps giving even more! When you decide to parent consciously, you have the opportunity to end any cycle of abuse that might have occurred with your parents or their parents and much further back. One client whom we'll call "John" came to discover the cause of a single issue, the anger he felt toward himself regarding his father. Together we discovered it and he healed it. Three months later I worked with John's first-born son to discover the root of the exact same issue. Another three months passed and I met John's father. I was not surprised to find the same pivotal issue of rejection in his script. John's wife studied the family history and concluded from her research this same breakdown between father and first-born son had existed for seven generations!

CHAPTER TWELVE

The World Needs Conscious You!

What a gift you are to a world in need of more conscious people who want to make a positive difference for themselves and for others! Those who make self-discovery and self-improvement a priority are lights in a darkness caused by fear, despair, blame, and hatred. You now know that whatever the limitation in your life, you made it up and can stop believing it!

The Body Memory Process assists you with moving a huge part of what has been blocking a more magnificent you. It is a conscious choice that will become a part of your healthy lifestyle. It is, however, not a "one and done" deal. In order to consistently see the rewards of a conscious life you must remain conscious from moment-to-moment, day-to-day. You will be able to use what you learned here again in the future.

What follows is a summary of the major points from this book, followed by a checklist that I suggest you post on your bathroom mirror or refrigerator so that you can see it often. I cannot stress enough the importance of reviewing this list every day to remain vigilant in a world that can be overwhelming and distracting to your commitment to remain conscious of your thoughts, words, and beliefs.

REMIND YOURSELF EVERY DAY...

1. I am a spiritual being having a human experience.

2. I choose to listen to my body's cues for what it needs and clues about whether there might be an imbalance to correct.

3. I choose to remain vigilant to patterns in my behavior, the way I communicate with others, and the way I receive communication from others.

4. For all my aspirations, I choose to remain inspired by focusing on my journey as well as the destination.

5. I choose to surrender to my own intuition and wisdom, trusting it will lead me to where I want to go.

6. I choose to remember the power of my thoughts and words and use words that empower my life and reflect the results I want.

7. I choose to not blame others for what shows up in my life and will always look for the lesson and the possible hidden vow.

8. I choose wellness in mind, body, and spirit.

9. I choose to only interact with children in a way that empowers them.

10. I choose to be an example of the power of conscious living in the world.

I am a spiritual being having a human experience.

It is important to remember every day that you are a spiritual being having a human experience. Too often, people are surprised when they have a spiritual experience. When you come to accept that you are truly a spiritual being living on Earth as a human, spiritual experiences will become the norm and they will guide you to a positive, fulfilling life. Everything in life vibrates at a certain level and you attract into your life that which vibrates at your level of thought and word. When you study and understand spiritual laws of attraction and manifestation, you will elevate your human experience.

I choose to listen to my body's cues for what it needs and clues to where there might be an imbalance to correct.

When you begin treating your body as your friend instead of your enemy, you will find yourself listening to essential information that will help keep you healthy. If you do find yourself in a water, electrolyte, nutrient, or hormonal imbalance, you will be able to make a correction before it progresses to disease. You will also notice when you need to stretch and exercise, when you need more sleep, when you need a chiropractic adjustment, and so much more. If you have ever visited a naturopathic doctor who uses natural remedies, you might have experienced muscle testing. This is because your body always knows and tells the truth! Remember, your body is your subconscious mind and can be your most valuable resource—if you allow it.

I choose to remain vigilant to patterns in my behavior, the way I communicate with others, and the way I receive communication from others.

A major clue to hidden childhood vows is whether your life is in balance. If you notice personal behavior patterns that annoy you and interfere with the outcomes you desire, there could be a hidden vow to discover. If you notice that you say or do something in a certain way to get what you want, you may get what you want, but you could be damaging your relationships. There could be a vow in place about what you need to do to get your way. Or if you have a certain negative emotional response to being told you are anything less than perfect, you might want to explore for a hidden vow about needing to "perfect" or "right."

For all my aspirations, I choose to remain inspired by focusing on my journey as well as the destination.

Being overly goal-oriented tends to put you into the future and out of the moment. It is important to take the time every day to  meditate on the future you choose to create. This entails you making a conscious choice in the present moment and is a very powerful way to create a life that is joyful and prosperous. It is possible to become discouraged when you are not meeting your goals as quickly as you would like. This robs you of the joy of being in the moment and recognizing that everything is as it should be, no matter where you are along your journey. Being too goal-focused also keeps you in a conditional state of mind that makes you believe you will be happy only if and when you meet your goal. By focusing on the journey, you can remain positive, knowing that the opposite is actually true. You will meet your goal when you live in the joy and knowing that the end result is already yours—it just needs the necessary time to unfold.

I choose to surrender to my own intuition and wisdom, trusting it will lead me to where I want to go.

This is closely related to being in tune with your journey to your destination. You should avoid focusing only on your initially chosen destination, ignoring the new data coming from your intuition, meditations, and your body. This can inform the direction you take and the things you do from day to day to meet that desired outcome—or perhaps lead you to an even more desirable outcome!

I choose to remember the power of my thoughts and words and use only words that empower my life and reflect the results I want.

In the hands of your very young, pre-logical, egocentric self, your thoughts and words were charged with your emotions and created the strong beliefs we call vows, hidden from you for years. Now that you are aware of how vows are created and how to discover and release them, you can consciously make these powerful tools called beliefs work for you! By remembering every day the power of your thoughts and words, and using only the words which empower you and bring energy to your dreams, you are creating the life you want.

I choose to not blame others for what shows up in my life and will always look for the lesson and the possible hidden vow.

Before people are aware of the power they wield to create their own reality, it is understandable that they might blame the government, their clergy, their parents, their teachers, their spouse, their children, the media or anything else outside themselves for the undesirable results in their life. Now that you are aware that you are the cause of the good, the bad, and the ugly, there is no way to start to blame anyone or anything else without perhaps getting a chuckle from your temporary slip. As David Sohn used to say, "There's no cheese in that tube!" which refers to how a lab mouse learns that there is no reward by going in a certain direction in the maze. There is no personal reward from blaming anyone but yourself. And there is no need to blame yourself for anything, because in the past, you did the best you could with the knowledge you had. Simply be conscious (recognize you are in charge of your reality), take action (change your thoughts and words, disavow any discovered vows), and move on.

I choose wellness in mind, body, and spirit.

You will find that it is difficult to choose wellness in one area of your life and neglect another. Pursuit of wellness is its own reward, and you will love the energy and the happiness that will result from vigilance regarding what you consume, what you think and say, and how you interact with and treat others.

I choose to only interact with children in a way that empowers them.

As we discussed in chapter eleven, if you interact with children in any way, it is important to realize the amazing impact you can have on their highly impressionable selves. It only takes one emotionally charged event for a child to form a vow that can burden them far into their future. As much potential as you have to harm a child with the way you speak to and treat them, you have to empower and make a lasting positive impression on them!

I choose to be an example of the power of conscious living in the world.

The world needs conscious you!

In this book you have learned how living consciously is a powerful way to create what you want. Let us conclude by taking a look at a world in need of people just like you.

I've shared my story about my difficult birth and how my healing has led me to now consider myself a "wounded healer." You too have a story about your life before you were conscious and after your awakening—which wasn't necessarily because of this book. What you learned here might just add to your ever-deepening understanding of yourself and what you can bring to the world to make it a happier, healthier, more peaceful place.

What I want you to know is if you are willing to share it, the world can benefit from your story. You are a living example that people do not need to remain stuck in a life that doesn't work well for them. You are a beacon of hope, having created beliefs when you were young, had a period of time when you weren't aware you had these vows, experienced limitations and issues because of those beliefs, then discovered and released your life-limiting vows. Upon reading this chapter, you might not yet have experienced the positive changes in your life that come with letting go of limiting beliefs, but they will come.

Who needs your example? We've discussed the impact you can have on children in your life. You will also be able to communicate more effectively with your spouse, your friends, your boss, and your work colleagues. Where before they might have been blurred, now the lines between what you manifest and what is manifested by others will be much clearer. You won't blame yourself for the unconscious behavior of others and you won't blame others for your own limitations. In your own style and in a way of your own choosing, you will create a better world because you have created a better you.

When you were very young and not yet logical, you made it up in a way that didn't work well for you. Do the work to stop believing it.

Now make it up the way you want and start believing it!

Notes

[i] Gilbert, Scott. "When Does Personhood Begin?" *News & Events :: Swarthmore College*, September 26, 2018. https://www.swarthmore.edu/news-events/when-does-personhood-begin.

[ii] Coleman, Kara, and Jennifer Villa. "Researchers Explore the Science behind the Maternal-Fetal Bond." *The Pew Charitable Trusts*. The Pew Charitable Trusts, November 12, 2020. https://pew.org/2GWXla0.

[iii] "About the CDC-Kaiser Ace Study |Violence Prevention|injury Center|CDC." *Centers for Disease Control and Prevention*. Centers for Disease Control and Prevention, April 6, 2021. https://www.cdc.gov/violenceprevention/aces/about.html.

[iv] Hay, Louise L. Essay. In *You Can Heal Your Life*. Bath: Camden, 2008.

[v] Leboyer Frédérick, and Yvonne Fitzgerald. *Birth without Violence*. London: Pinter & Martin, 2011.

[vi] Verny, Thomas R. *Secret Life of the Unborn Child: How You Can Prepare Your Baby for a Happy, Healthy Life*. SIMON & SCHUSTER, 2019.

[vii] Love, Patricia, and Jo Robinson. *The Emotional Incest Syndrome: What to Do When a Parent's Love Rules Your Life*. New York: Bantam Books, 1991.

Free Gift!

Please download your free gift at the Body Memory Process website:
https://bodymemoryprocess.com/youmadeitup/freedownload
You will receive:

- Summary sheets for the Body Memory Process homework

- A sheet for your discovered vows!

- Ten Reminders for Conscious Living Every Day

Made in the USA
Columbia, SC
11 August 2024

39786995R00087